NAVIGATING DEVOPS THROUGH WATERFALLS

Navigating DevOps Through Waterfalls

First published: November 2020

ISBN: 978-1999529109

https://www.tactec.ca

In thirty years of business and IT I have never stopped learning from others, even what may be considered old ideas. A big thanks to all those I have worked with in the industry! For my wife Dawn who has brought unnumbered cups of tea and lunch when I lost track of time at sea, I could not do this without your support!

ᑕᑎᐯᎥ ↓ΞᐯᎥ ᛘᐃ7ᐟᐯᎥ ᐃᛕ ↓ΞᐯᎥ ᖴᐯᎩᐃᑕᐟᐴ ᑕᐟᐴ7ᐴᐯᎥ↓

Brent A. Reed

I secretly hope that someday, my daughter Noya willingly reads this book.

0x53 0x65 0x63 0x72 0x65 0x74 0x20 0x53 0x61 0x75 0x63 0x65

Mathew Mathai

A call out and thank you to every engineer who inspires others to continuously learn and share. My gratitude to my wife Carola and three boys Alexander, Jacques, and Thorsten who are my sunshine, lighthouse and harbour as they continue to support and tolerate my turbulent binary adventures. As promised (before), this is the last trek that inspires a book.

-.. . ...- --- .--. ... / -- .. -. -.. ... . -

Willy-Peter Schaub

Contents

Foreword

DevOps has become table stakes for modern organisations. DevOps must be baked right into your organizational Way of Working (WoW) if you are to thrive in the "new normal" of constant change. DevOps enables your teams to become semi-autonomous, self-organizing and more disciplined in their WoW with a better position to improve how they address the needs of their customers. This book provides proven strategies to make this happen.

The authors present their DevOps adoption advice as a story. This is a tale of a fateful trip, a trip that started from a tropic isle, aboard a tiny ship. The mate was a mighty sailing man, the skipper brave and sure. Five passengers set sail that day for a three-hour tour. A three-hour tour! But the weather started getting rough, the tiny ship was tossed. If not for the courage of the fearless crew, they would have been lost! Oh wait, that's Gilligan's Island, not this story. My bad.

This book is a story based on the hard-won experiences of the four authors after helping various organizations for years in their DevOps adoptions. DevOps has effectively become table stakes for your organization's IT processes, even more so given how COVID-19 has upended societies around the globe. In the private sector, the marketplace has become far more competitive, requiring companies to get better at sensing and responding quickly to meet their customers' needs before someone else does. In the public sector, the needs of their citizens have increased while the tax base has shrunk, implying that they need to do more with less. My advice is to take this book seriously – although it is presented as a work of fiction, the lessons in it are very real and very important.

Now that I think about it, many DevOps adoption efforts turn out to be a lot like Gilligan's Island. Many organizations mistakenly believe at first that they are embarking on a short effort to adopt DevOps or, worse yet, to "install" DevOps. They hope that their journey will be straightforward and over quickly, perhaps three to six months to Gilligan's three hours. However, they quickly find themselves in trouble, stuck on a transformation trip that they don't know how to navigate.

Why do DevOps transformation efforts run into problems? It's often because they don't invest the time to identify a compelling vision and, instead, head out into the transformation sea. A critical lesson that the authors convey in their tale is that you must define, and then communicate clearly and consistently, both the *what* and the *why* of your DevOps transformation. Your objectives and the results you hope to achieve become a driving force for your organizational success and a driver for your metrics. What gets measured will improve, and it is not uncommon to have many things that need to do so in order to fulfill your goals.

There are other similarities between ineffective DevOps transformations and Gilligan's Island. Many episodes centered around some sort of unlikely strategy for the castaways to escape their predicament, but their plan would invariably fail due to mis-execution. Sometimes the professor's attempts to cobble together the existing material available to him – bamboo, coconuts, and something that had recently washed ashore – would fail because they simply were not up to the task. Sometimes the castaways would have different personal goals, working at odds to one another. Other times, one of the castaways, usually Gilligan, would make a mistake and ruin the plan.

Just like the castaways were thrown into a situation that they were ill-equipped to deal with, many DevOps transformations are poorly thought through. When funding for new tooling is not available and teams are forced to make do with what they have, this is the equivalent of the professor trying to cobble together a radio from coconuts and bamboo. When teams do not know the *what* and *why* of your strategy, they work at odds to one another and waste organizational resources. When people lack training and coaching in new DevOps techniques and technologies they are apt to make mistakes that will undermine your organization's efforts to escape from their existing WoW.

But I digress. The entire predicament of having to escape from Gilligan's Island could have been completely avoided had they only known what they were doing to begin with. First, they would have acted differently had they been aware that they were going out into a storm. And let me be clear about this, DevOps transformations always get stormy. The advice described in this book shows you how to avoid common problems that other organizations have suffered from and how to navigate through them.

Second, if they had a better boat and a crew prepared for the situation that they faced then they, very likely, could have successfully weathered the storm. This book works through the equivalent of building a capable crew by describing the mindset and skillset needed to succeed. This includes business representatives that are actively involved in the effort and a supportive engineering process (or at least the beginnings of one). It also shows how to build a better boat by picking the right project(s) and developing a supporting DevOps infrastructure.

Third, you need some outside help. Just as the castaways on Gilligan's Island faced problems that they were incapable of overcoming on their own, so will you. The transformation journey described in this book is supported by experienced change agents who coach the organization along the way. Without such help you will quickly find your transformation efforts running aground on the shoals of organizational complexities you do not know how to avoid on your own.

Regardless of where you are on your DevOps adoption journey, even if you are far down the path and realise that you are actually on a continuous improvement journey, this book has something for you. I learned a fair bit by reading this, and I've been doing this for years.

Scott Ambler
Vice President and Chief Scientist, Disciplined Agile
October 2020

Act 0

DevOps is Key

The Overlords

It was a warm autumn day. Birds chirped outside the Leaders Retreat, a wooden structure high in the mountains, far away from the hustle and bustle of the office. Inside, the crackling sound of electricity bounced off sparks of silver light, dancing between pink, pulsating brains, hovering together. The Overlords' minds were sharpened and poised, deciding on the plans and goals for the year ahead.

Bobbing up and down in their glass shells, they agreed that performance was key to bringing value to and retaining the customers that seemed to be leaving in droves.

After much discussion, they identified the increase in performance issues was due to the poor delivery and quality of the painfully slow IT Department, noting that costs were also increasing while customer and business unit satisfaction steadily declined. Yet, the Overlords, considered masters of the corporation, wondered how to reverse this trajectory and attract more customers than ever before.

"Why is this happening?" they pondered aloud in unison. *"Why isn't our Digital Transformation plan working?"*

Maverick, the astute IT CIO, sensing the Overlords' frustration, began writing on the whiteboard:

DevOps is key to unlocking IT performance.

This stopped the discussion, and Maverick said, with complete confidence, *"Our competitors are implementing their digital strategy quicker and more cost-effectively with DevOps, using Agile processes."*

This sparked the group's interest. They asked Maverick several questions, but he was unable to elaborate further on the topic. They all wanted to know more, prompting them to research 'DevOps Performance' online for more information. When presented with the thousands of related search results, they decided to read through the Report from DevOps Research and Assessment (DORA) (DORA, 2014-2019), the first link in the array of resources.

Almost instantly, their cerebral discussion reignited with jolts of lightning as they realised that Maverick was on to something!

"This report says that DevOps will fix our problems!" they stated, enthusiastically.

The Overlords and Maverick began chanting, *"DevOps, DevOps, DevOps!"* although none fully understood what it was. However, they believed it could be the silver bullet to their delivery, quality, and performance issues, and possibly even the solution to their struggling IT department!

Maverick, feeling as if he just won the lottery, thought to himself, *"I better get to the DevOps Conference quickly and figure out how to get this Agile and DevOps integrated into my teams, pronto!"*

***

A few days later, at the DevOps Worldwide Conference hosted by Computer Corp, making his way through the myriad of booths full of swag, he spied a relaxing spot with some refreshments. As he approached, he overheard a group engaged in light conversation to the side of the table.

"Yeah, someone told me today they could cure cancer with DevOps!" one of the four Agents joked, resulting in laughter all around. Maverick poured himself a drink then walked over to introduce himself. Upon doing so, he learned that this was not just any group but a group of experts, known as the Agents of Chaos (AoCs).

Agent 13 explained, *"My colleagues and I are DevOps enthusiasts, so to speak. We are laughing about how DevOps is supposed to cure everything, and any CIO can just buy it off the shelf."*

Smiling, Agent 77 chimed in, *"Yeah, if you take a quick look around, you can see how confused people are about what DevOps is. In fact, many think it is a product or CIO edict."*

"And some think of it as a miracle. DevOps can't cure stupid!" Agent 9 added with a smirk.

Maverick was impressed. *"So, you guys know how to deliver DevOps?"* he asked, hopefully.

"We always do our best," Agent 13 assured. *"Each of us has been in one or more roles within a company that has successfully implemented DevOps for the interim or part of the journey."*

"How long does DevOps take?" inquired Maverick, pleased to have stumbled upon these experts.

"Well it's a continuous journey of improvement, so it never ends," Agent 77 informed.

Maverick took a moment to contemplate this before asking the AoCs, *"Would you be willing to help my company deliver DevOps to help fix our IT problems?"*

The AoCs looked at one another and replied together, *"Sure, why not!"*

The group exchanged contact information before disbursing. Maverick could not believe his luck and hurried through the rest of the day's events, excited to share the news with his team.

As soon as he got back to his hotel room, he went straight for his laptop to send an email to the IT Manager.

```
Barker,

Do you remember when we discussed making DevOps
one of our key priorities? Today I met a group
called the Agents of Chaos (AoCs), and I think
they are who can help us get us out of our IT
mess and accelerate our plans for DevOps. I would
like you to meet them next week to get started on
the DevOps adoption project. Their contact
information is attached. Please set something up
to initiate the process.

-M
```

Barker, who was in the middle of a meeting with this team, saw the message pop up on his watch. The news energised him, and he decided to announce it immediately.

"Everyone, I just received a very exciting email. We are going to do a new, high-priority project called 'DevOps Adoption'. We believe this will transform our IT department, making us all heroes! So, get ready to become Agile and do DevOps!"

The team looked up at him, wide-eyed.

"The order just came in from Maverick, who is on his way back from a DevOps conference," he informed. *"He engaged Agile DevOps experts who have committed to helping us with this transformation. This is top priority, everyone!"* Standing up to emphasise the importance of this directive, he instructed, *"Be prepared to focus solely on this when they arrive next week!"*

Meanwhile, in a small tavern down the road from the conference, the AoCs were sipping their favourite golden elixir, discussing the potential challenges and nuances of handling this adoption and transformation at Big Corp. Although they were accustomed to the common challenges centered on the existing organisational culture and mindset, they knew that asking tough questions and working to resolve the answers meant disruption and chaos.

They prepared themselves to "poke the hornets' nest" with the understanding that the questions, answers and solutions meant having difficult conversations to enforce real change.

The AoCs had not earned their moniker randomly though. All four were fully aware that they were disruptors against the traditional norm, each in their own way. While Agent 77 promoted an Agile hybrid toolkit called Disciplined Agile and DevOps (DAD), and Agent 13 supported a less formal, more pragmatic approach based on simplicity, Agent 9 questioned the intent and value of everything involved in the existing processes, encouraging organisations to reflect on areas of improvements. Agent 14, the quiet scribe and illustrator, tended to remain in the background, capturing the mood, context and nuances of key situations he observed.

Despite the difference in each Agent's focus, all were open-minded and passionate with a shared goal of delighting their stakeholders. They always tried to enable and bring joy to organisations, leadership, and engineering teams.

As a group, the AoCs decided to establish a set of "Core Values" to support their chaotic ways. They developed and agreed upon five standards to sum up how adopting the DevOps mindset would bring value and aid the change. These also served to set expectations for their clients during the process of finding solutions to some of the significant challenges they all faced.

They were:

1. **Value stakeholders and their feedback** rather than simply adapting to change.

2. **Strive to always innovate and improve** beyond repeatable processes and frameworks.

3. **Inspire and share collaboratively** instead of becoming a hero or silo.

4. **Measure performance across the organisation** not just a line of business.

5. **Create a culture of learning through Lean quality deliverables** over tools and automation.

Journey Format

"Hi, readers! I'm Agent 77, and I thought I would introduce you to the format of this book since it is slightly different from its counterparts. There are five Acts, consisting of a(n):

- *Morning chat with various characters, including our very own AoCs!*
- *Main story line, where we see each character enter as the story develops. A small picture is displayed the first time a new character appears.*
- *Interaction between the AoCs about a particular topic.*
- *Afternoon huddle.*
- *Team chat, where we discuss what occurred within.*
- *Summary with an observation of an unspoken pattern you may recognise from personal experience."*

Act 1

ASSESS - Be Agile, do DevOps!

A Morning Chat

It was a sunny morning and the start of the first day with Big Corp. Agents 9 and 13 walked from the harbour to meet Agent 77 on his way for their ten o'clock meeting with Maverick and Barker. Agent 9 was in his usual, energetic mode.

"All I'm saying is, if you hear a DevOps enthusiast's view, you'd believe it was the answer for everything. The DevOps extremist would make you think it could end terrorism (pun intended)!" He paused briefly. *"DevOps may be the solution to a lot of problems, but it certainly isn't the answer to them all!"*

Both Agents of Chaos laughed. They had heard the hype, but neither could pinpoint how DevOps had earned it. They understood how **dev**elopment and **op**eration**s** teams working together could create success, but since DevOps was often used, incorrectly, as a synonym for the Agile methodology, many questions needed to be answered and concepts clarified. For example:

- Is DevOps a set of Agile tools, a separate methodology or both?
- Was the current IT world so troubled that it justified looking for a knight in shining armor or a silver bullet?
- Are IT projects that use DevOps guaranteed for success?
- Are IT projects using Waterfall doomed for failure?
- Can IT companies efficiently provide any value to their end customers without DevOps?
- Were there any other ways for development and operations teams to collaborate without using DevOps?

They agreed to prioritise clearly defining the overloaded and misunderstood term 'DevOps', discussing ways to do so on the way to their meeting.

We Need DevOps! Make It So!

While waiting for the AoCs to arrive, Maverick unpacked all the information gathered on his conference trip. Motivated by the annual retreat with the Overlords, he had been sure to take every opportunity to attend the various presentations by leading software companies where he was witness to many polished slides on DevOps and the benefits of Agile adoption in companies looking to achieve digital transformation fast and furiously.

One presentation highlighted their enhanced ability to routinely deploy hundreds of feature updates per day in production for their early adopters sometimes affectionately called canaries, using their One Engineering System (Microsoft, 1ES, 2020). Another discussed the support for business leaders and technologists articulating a taxonomy, common lexicon and set of metrics to measure the business value using the Flow Framework (Tasktop, 2020).

Maverick knew that his organisation was in dire need of a change in order to compete with the competition. They needed to go faster and improve both the performance and quality of their continuous innovations and core solutions.

After digesting the State of DevOps Report (Puppet, 2019) and Executive Guide to Disciplined Agile (Ambler, Scott W., 2019), he realised DevOps really might make all the difference in his department's performance and culture. Maverick saw the benefits of having goals and following sensible principles. He knew Barker would be less excited about changing the culture since he preferred immediate results, but he also knew Barker would be supportive of improving the flow and being enterprise aware despite his impatience with certain principles, such as delighting the customer.

Maverick particularly liked a principle that emphasised the importance of context and not being prescriptive, thinking that those may be large contributors to why they failed.

"Perhaps, our processes are too rigid," he thought.

Thus, he needed to get Barker focused on what Barker did best while leveraging help from the AoCs to drive the principles and goals that made sense.

Barker walked into the office and sat down, dropping a worn copy of the State of DevOps 2019 report onto his desk.

"Wow! Did you see the performance numbers DevOps is supposed to give?"

Maverick had not gotten to that point in his reading yet. He flipped a few pages and quickly skimmed the report.

"Very impressive!" Maverick said with a smile, knowing that it would drive Barker towards implementing DevOps. They both reviewed the comparison of low performers against elite teams, which seemed too good to be true. Together they found that the top performers had:

- 46 times greater **Deployment Frequency**, making the introduction of new value into production mode quicker.
- 7 times lower **Change Failure Rate**, reducing rework and allowing focus on new value.
- 2,555 times faster **Lead Time for Change**, enabling quicker feedback and more effective outage responses.
- 2,604 times faster **Mean Time to Recover**, mitigating failures more rapidly to provide users higher availability.

Barker, excited by the performance potential and statistics, missed a crucial factor that Maverick had not. Several pages later it was spelled out in black and white; *culture, safety, sustainability*. These, and other people factors, directly affected performance.

Maverick looked at Barker, scanning the data collected over many years, and saw his contempt.

"Well, we cannot argue with the data. There is something to be said about the need to be supported and motivated to perform, Barker!" he pointed out.

"Yes, yes," Barker dismissed, not subscribing to the concept of people and culture needing to feel safe. He was only interested in fast results, especially if his staff wanted to keep their jobs!

Maverick wasted no time, getting right to the point.

"Barker, I had a phenomenal trip. During our company retreat with the Overlords then at the DevOps Conference, I was privileged to gather invaluable learnings and useful information. I believe we have the Overlords' full support as they are committed to implementing Agile and DevOps in our IT department. We need to install these methodologies into the process! In fact, I have to give the directors an Agile DevOps transformation plan by next Monday."

Barker's mind reeled. He wondered if this meant developing a completely new department. If so, with more staff under his control, he could show the other IT managers who Maverick's best go-to man was!

"Wow, no pressure!" Barker exclaimed. *"So, does this mean that, with DevOps, we will have to merge development and operation teams?"*

"First things first, Barker," Maverick said.

They sat there for a prolonged period of silence before hearing the AoCs arrive.

"I think we are ready for these miracle workers," Barker said in anticipation.

What is DevOps?

Maverick's head bustled with information, three-letter acronyms (TLAs) and jargon from the recent briefings. Between self-organizing teams, organisational tractors, blast radiuses, deploy <> release, dark launches, Feature Flags, pipelines, technical debt, and Agile <> DevOps, he did not know where to begin.

"Agents, where should we start?" he asked. *"Perhaps with the definition of DevOps?"*

Agent 77 smiled and explained that DevOps is an overloaded term, so clearly defining it is precisely the right place to start. Everyone in the room laughed, except Barker.

"So, what is YOUR definition of it then?" he scoffed.

Agent 13 replied, *"There are so many! Some seem to promise a silver bullet or make DevOps sound like rocket science where others try selling a product or framework."* He stopped, the smile fading from his face.

"Wow, you sound agitated!" Barker remarked.

"Sorry, I just believe that DevOps is a healthy mindset, not a product you can buy or install, nor is it new. In fact, in the early 1980s, my first mentor instilled in me several software engineering practises that have re-emerged with DevOps.

"Agent 77 will walk you through the DevOps manifesto we created with the community to encourage a consistent message," he said while regaining his composure. *"He can give the definition of* Disciplined DevOps *(Ambler, Scott W., 2020). I know he is very passionate about it."*

Agent 13 gave him the floor, but before Agent 77 could open his mouth, Maverick interjected.

"Oh, I just read that in the beginning chapter of the DA Executive Guide you kindly gave me!"

Agent 77 smiled, gesturing for Maverick to continue.

"Hmmm, if I recall correctly, it is a streamlining of IT solution development and operations."

His face appeared to be requesting confirmation, so Agent 77 added, *"...and supporting enterprise-IT activities to provide more effective outcomes to an organisation."*

Maverick nodded in relief. *"Exactly,"* he said.

"However, there is more than one definition, even among us AoCs, but we all agree with the principle," Agent 77 acknowledged.

"Aha!" Barker exclaimed. *"I knew you guys could not define it!"*

This made Agent 77 shake his head and Agent 9 laugh.

"Actually, we all agree. We just add our own perspective and context to it as well," Agent 77 clarified.

"*Right,*" Agent 13 agreed. "*That is why I prefer the definition by Donovan Brown, stating that DevOps is the union of people, process, and products to enable continuous delivery of value to our end users* (Brown, 2015)."

"*Yes! Value!*" Maverick cried out. "*I like that!*"

Barker, prompted by the enthusiasm, exclaimed, "*Union of processes! Process and governance, I say!*"

Everyone was nodding as Agent 13 took his laptop out of his bag. "*Here, let me show you.*"

He flipped open his laptop and showed Maverick and Barker a recording from a recent event where Donovan elaborated on his definition of DevOps.

"*I am very deliberate in the terms used in this definition. I choose value over software. DevOps is not just automating a pipeline, so we can quickly deliver software. Our goal is to deliver value. The term end users was also very carefully chosen. The value we produce must reach our end users. If the value reaches the Dev and QA environments but is held up before reaching production to be realised by our end users, we are still failing.*

"*It is very important to realise that DevOps is not a product. You cannot buy and install DevOps. It is not just automation or infrastructure as code. DevOps is people following a process enabled by products to deliver value to our end users.*"

The recording resonated with Barker and Maverick.

"*Delight the customer,*" Maverick stated, summarizing his main takeaway.

The AoCs smiled, satisfied with their progress and the level of comprehension. Barker looked at his watch, feeling pleased with the amount of information already covered. He had no idea it was time to shift left, from departments to the business, but the AoCs knew that was the next step.

Business Values

"It is time to discuss value from the business perspective," Agent 13 informed the leadership duo.

"Business? I thought DevOps is for IT. We do not need to talk about the business side. They are a pain and never know what they want," Barker objected.

Maverick looked at Barker, nodding in agreement. He was not sure how this all fit in either.

"Yes, please explain where business value in DevOps is important," he requested.

"Let us look at one aspect," Agent 13 began, taking a deep breath. *"These days, organisations are moving from a resource-optimized business model based on capital expenses (CAPEX) toward a market-optimized model based on operational expenses (OPEX). To remain competitive and respond to rapidly changing business and technology trends, as well as regulatory and compliance requirements, you must find ways to:*

- *Ship value! – Increase the delivery of value to customers.*
- *Ship value faster! – Shorten the delivery cycle.*
- *Ship the right value faster! – Monitor, learn, adapt, and pivot.*
- *Ship the right and better value faster! – Improve quality!*
- *Ship the right and better value faster while reducing cost and efficiency! – Reduce cost and simplify through automation."*

Barker and Maverick liked what they were hearing.

"You mentioned quality. Our department has had many discussions with our business stakeholders and engineering department about this. We cannot seem to come to an agreement on whether the feature or quality is more important. What is your take on this matter?" Barker asked, hoping for guidance.

The AoCs paused for a moment and exchanged several looks. Finally, Agent 77 blurted out, *"Oh boy! This is certainly a good topic, but it is also a complex one! May I suggest we table it and discuss in more detail later when we have dedicated time to do so?"*

Agent 13, looking slightly humbled, added, *"I am an engineer at heart and always argue that quality is non-negotiable. However, it requires an investment in continuous dedication, commitment, learning, training, process, and products. Quality delivers business benefits such as delighted customers, effective development processes, better predictability, performance, reliability, innovation, and compliance."*

Agent 77 raised his eyebrows as if to confirm the solid point Agent 13 made. *"I agree, however, as an Enterprise Architect, using the principle of being pragmatic, you can reach a point when adding more quality may surpass value."* He stopped for a moment to organise his thoughts. *"Of course, it depends on whether you are building lifesaving medical equipment, aircraft parts or customer feedback forms. In any case, I go with the idea of JBGE."*

Maverick and Barker exchanged puzzled glances.

*"**Just barely good enough** (JBGE). Basically, you iterate on your quality and stop when it no longer adds additional value,"* Agent 9 explained.

This cleared up the confusion for the two, who nodded in understanding. The picture was becoming clearer, and they both wanted to learn more. Barker even smiled (a rare event in itself)! The passion and straightforward logic of the AoCs worked well with Maverick and Barker's mindset. It kept them engaged and eager to continue moving forward.

The clock on the wall chimed, reminding them to take a break.

"Let's grab a coffee then discuss the people aspect of all this when we reconvene," Maverick proposed. *"I'd like hear you explain why the 'State of the Union Report' and 'Executive Guide to Disciplined Agile' emphasise awesome people, culture, and safety."*

Barker frowned. *"Yeah, I wondered about that as well,"* he admitted.

"Sounds like a plan," Agent 9 said, standing up to stretch his legs. The group disbursed to the breakroom and bathroom to get resituated for the next round of discussion.

Transformation Turbulence and Rapids

Twenty minutes later, Maverick, Barker and the AoCs were settled and ready to resume. Agent 13 started off by addressing why one of the biggest challenges is an organisation's **people** and **culture**.

"The AoCs have seen, first-hand, the need to create a supportive leadership, one which accepts failure, and inspires and stimulates the organisation. It is also imperative to nurture empowered teams that are not afraid of continuous learning or failure."

He flipped through his notebook and withdrew a survey he had referenced, handing copies to Maverick and Barker. After scanning the report, they were impressed with its contents, particularly Figure 1, which Agent 13 had created.

"Hard data, Barker!" said Maverick, emphatically, after absorbing the information. *"This proves it! The community agrees that the hardest challenge of a DevOps transformation is the **people**! That tops the other challenges by a mile!"*

Rank	Options	First choice ▪ ▪ Last choice
1	People	
1	Process	
2	Products	

Figure 1 – Community poll: Which of these is the hardest challenge of a DevOps transformation?

The AoCs were pleased that Maverick seemed to get it *and* be completely on board. Barker, on the other hand, sat there, looking slightly stunned.

"Well, I guess I cannot argue with these new wonder kids?" Barker huffed, shrugging his shoulders.

"Hard data, Barker. Hard data," Maverick repeated.

The group continued their discussion until it was time for lunch. Maverick ushered everyone out of his office, saying to the AoCs, *"We will definitely chat soon. Barker plans to introduce you to the team after lunch. I have an important meeting with Finance, so I shall check back with you later."* He shook their hands and returned to his office to prepare for his meeting.

"Follow me, Agents. Let's meet the team first!" beckoned Barker who, after looking over the AoCs to ensure they have their Big Corp visitor badges on, straightened Agent 77's before proceeding down the hallway.

Agent 13 looked over at Agent 77. *"I do hope we get lunch soon,"* he whispered. *"I am famished!"*

Effective Teams

Barker led the AoCs to Big Corps' cafeteria where they found seats around a table in the corner near a window with plenty of space and far enough away to allow them to chat without noise or interruption. While they waited for everyone to filter in for lunch, Barker imagined what the organisation would look like after the transformation, what his team size would be and who would become his DevOps champions.

"Tell me, Agent 77, you didn't say much about the people aspect. Are you aligned with your colleagues on this?" Barker asked in earnest.

Agent 77 felt certain he had mentioned how important people are and will always be, particularly to a DevOps transformation. One of the things he learned over the years was to watch and observe people's reactions, especially when a giant stick was poking them, a hornet's nest, or both! Agent 77 noticed that Barker flinched every time Maverick mentioned *people* or *proof* or *hard data.* In fact, at times he looked downright uncomfortable. Agent 77 made a note about how much of a sticking point this seemed to be for Barker and so early in the process to boot! All the AoCs had noticed his rather controlling and mechanical managerial qualities.

"Barker is a command and control type of manager," Agent 77 thought to himself. He was brought back to the conversation when he heard, *"Agent..."* and saw Barker looking him straight in the eye.

He refocused and replied thoughtfully.

*"I agree with my colleagues. Agent 13 is spot on that it takes the leadership and staff cooperatively engaging in the right team environment ... in other words **people** and **culture**."* Agent 77 stopped but quickly resumed when Barker continued staring at him, expectantly. *"Actually, one of our first goals in DevOps will be for you and Maverick to form an effective team that spans leadership, business, and engineering!"*

At this, Agents 9 and 13 quickly bit a mouthful of food in case Barker kicked them out of the cafeteria before they could finish eating. They chewed in hesitation, waiting for him to react.

Barker exhaled loudly. *"I suppose you are right,"* he admitted, breaking the tension. *"But I am really going to need your help with that,"* he added as if asking more than telling.

The AoCs saw this breakthrough with Barker as an opportunity to talk about **Effective Teams**.

Agent 9 led the conversation by quizzing Barker.

"Do any of these acronyms mean anything to you?
- *OeS*
- *CoE*
- *CoP*
- *DOaaS"*

As if reading Barker's mind, Agent 13 remarked, *"Do you not love TLAs? Oops, I mean three-lettered acronyms."*

Agent 9 chuckled. *"Jokes aside, you and your leadership team are a key enabler for a successful transformation. You need to establish an aspirational, inspiring, and achievable vision, respect for people, continuous flow of work, continuous innovation and learning, and a drive for relentless improvement."*

He ate his last bite of food then said, *"I read an interesting blog post, What Team Structure is Right for DevOps to Flourish* (Skelton, Matthew, 2013), *which discussed the possible need for organisations to have different team structures for effective Dev and Ops collaboration to take place.*

"Your organisation needs to express an achievable and shared goal for your digital transformation. There needs to be a common understanding of business, technology, value stream management, and, most importantly, a common business and technology language or lexicon spoken by everyone across departments.

"As per Figure 2, seamless and transparent collaboration between the development and operational engineering teams is critical, with

shared accountability and responsibility for the value streams from **ideation** *to* **deprecation**."

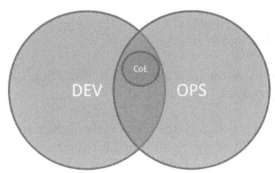

Figure 2 – Promised land of collaboration

"Which brings us to two of the acronyms you mentioned," Agent 13 injected.

"Yes, precisely," Agent 9 confirmed. *"A center of excellence (CoE) or DevOps-As-A-Service (DOaaS) team can help your organisation bridge the gap between DEV and OPS, translate operational, business and development language, mentor about automation, monitoring, testing and configuration management, and establish a common engineering system.*

"Both models fulfill an enablement role and must have a goal to make themselves obsolete as the organisation becomes DevOps savvy and mature."

How do CoE and DOaaS differ?

CoE implies maturity and is typically not a temporary team. Joined Community of Practises (CoP) can mature into CoE.

DOaaS is a third-party service provider that helps implement the necessary infrastructure and delivers DevOps guidance and mentorship.

"The other acronym, OeS, likely stands for One Engineering System, which we generally refer to as the Common Engineering System," Agent 13 explained. *"The idea is to create a collaboration system based on pillars, such as process, products, frameworks, and governance, which brings all stakeholders together in a transparent and collaborative environment."*

Barker soaked in all the information and found himself at a loss for words. *"Wow, thanks,"* he managed.

The AoCs could practically see the wheels turning in his brain. They hoped the information was saturating and that he was comprehending just how crucial all of this is to success.

"Can you walk me through your thoughts on an effective team?" he finally asked, eager to learn even more. The AoCs exchanged glances, and since Agent 13 had already finished his dessert, he spoke first.

"As discussed in our Blueprint for a team with a DevOps mindset article (Agent 13, 2018), *your organisation needs to influence through leadership and autonomy, promoting a culture of trust, learning and experimentation."*

Barker nodded, starting on his dessert.

Agent 13 continued, *"As shown in Figure 3, which everyone should tattoo on their forearm, the leadership owns the WHAT and WHY based on a clear definition of its vision, goals and governance. It is important that the leadership does not interfere below the line of autonomy and supports failure as an opportunity to reflect and improve without the fear of the 'big stick' persecution. Thus, when you hear some say, 'Fail Fast' what they mean is that, if you are going to fail, you want to do so initially and quickly.*

"In DevOps, failing sooner rather than later usually means improved quality and effectiveness because cost grows exponentially further into the development. Failing during a delivery phase

(iteration) becomes more expensive as you progress to the transition phase."

Agent 9 handed Barker a cool looking triangle sticker. Looking at it he said, *"Ah, now I understand why that triangle sticker is on each of your laptops!"*

Agent 9 smiled. *"Effective teams own their process. The **team** plans **who**, **when** and **how** the work will be accomplished to ensure it's aligned with organisational goals."*

Barker's eyes widened. *"The teams plan when..."* he whispered aloud in disbelief.

"See the sticker," Agent 9 pointed to the top of it. *"Here, above the line, your senior management team should define and enforce governance to ensure alignment with organisational, regulatory, legal, and ethical requirements and principles."*

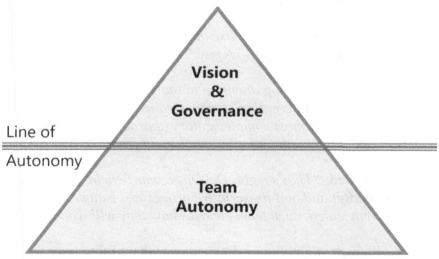

Figure 3 – Line of autonomy triangle

"Well, that makes total sense, and I 100% agree with the latter part of what you said." Barker seemed recharged. *"Leadership must own the **what** and **why**! However, I am not sure about the team owning*

the **how** and **when**. *How can that work?*" Barker asked, inquisitively.

"*Well,*" replied Agent 9. "*We encourage engineering teams below the line of autonomy to create manifestos to gradually influence the organisation's technical governance. It is about the right choice of words and tone. For example, manifesto sounds far less intimidating than standards or governance.*"

Barker made a face that acknowledged the point Agent 9 had made.

"*The concept of autonomy, self-organisation, self-management and cross-functionality is core to the practise of agility. In addition, a Lean practise promotes the reduction of waste through a short feedback loop and lightweight change approval while limiting work in progress (WIP), reflecting and acting on feedback and transparently visualizing work management. This means autonomy and responsibility, which helps build trust between leaders and teams,*" Agent 9 finished.

"*This is all great, but we do realise that we are talking about Agile, not DevOps right now. Right?*" Agent 77 cautioned.

"*Yes! Thank you for calling attention to that!*" Agent 9 exclaimed. "*We are talking about creating effective teams to get the benefits of DevOps. Agile is the most complementary approach, although Waterfall and other methodologies can benefit from DevOps too.*"

Agent 77 nodded. "*That's right, DevOps teams benefit greatly from an Agile mindset and non-prescriptive processes because, as Agent 13 and 9 both stated, each team chooses how they will work!*"

Barker, although slightly overwhelmed, was thankful to have the AoCs's expertise. He stood up and said, "*It doesn't look like we will be meeting the team during lunch, considering lunch is over!*" They all laughed. "*We have some time before our next meeting. Maverick has mentioned the terms self-organisation and self-management. Perhaps, we could head back to my office and you could expand on those a bit?*"

The AoCs nodded and followed Barker down the long corridors and up the stairs to his office.

"Thank goodness we took the stairs," Agent 9 said, exasperated. *"That was a huge lunch!"*
"Dessert certainly didn't help the matter!" laughed Agent 13 as he patted his full stomach.

Back in the office, the AoCs explained while Barker took notes, outlining the following:

- **Self-organisation** is a natural process that creates order within the team and key part to moving towards pulling work rather than being assigned or pushed work. It outlines how the autonomous team collaborates and coordinates.

- **Self-management** defines how the diverse team members work together in their own way, aligned with a shared vision and governance, owned by the leadership.

- **Effective teams** typically consist of **six to twelve** core or primary team **members** that enjoy working together. Most importantly, they passionately take ownership and accountability of their work from ideation to deprecation. They understand and embrace the opportunity of a journey with a destination they will never reach to continuously deliver value to their customers, organisation and engineering systems.

Agent 77 attached a drawing by Agent 13 (Figure 4) to Barker's meticulously clean whiteboard, using another magnetic 'Lines of Autonomy' sticker, like the one Agent 9 had given him over lunch.

Agent 13, proud of the usefulness of these visuals, described the images to the studious Barker, who continued scribbling down notes.

*"**Cross-functional** is another key part of genetic information for an effective team blueprint. Contrary to common belief, it does not imply that everyone on the team can do everything. Instead, as shown in Figure 4, the cross-functional team is based on the concept of T-shaped skills or T-shaped persons.*

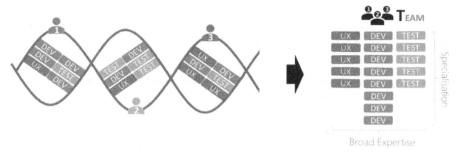

Figure 4 – T-shaped team and persons

"The horizontal bar of the T stands for broad expertise and the ability to collaborate with others while the vertical bar represents the depth of a single expertise." He paused to allow Barker time to jot it all down.

"Assume we have a three-person team made up of experts in development, testing and user experience. Each has his or her own T-shaped skills. When we combine the three experts' genetic material, we get a joint T-shaped team with specialization and broad ability that can design, develop, test and support features as a cross-functional team. These are some of the core strengths you will find in the genetic makeup of an effective team. Here is a blueprint you can cross-reference when you meet with yours," Agent 13 said as he handed Barker the paper.

"When teams work together with different skills they cross-pollenate, and each team member learns new skills, which broadens your team's and organisation's capability and scalability!" Agent 77 pointed out.

Barker loved the visuals and, surprisingly, had no issue with them being stuck smack in the middle of his pristine whiteboard.

Agent 9 resumed, *"I like the Dan Pink quote, 'To motivate employees who work beyond basic tasks, give them these three factors to increase performance and satisfaction: Autonomy, Mastery, and Purpose.'*

*"Look up '**The Surprising Truth About What Motivates Us** and **Dan Pink**'* (Pink, 2010). *The results will point you to a gobsmacking video that summarises many of the key concepts we discussed this morning."*

Agent 77 took out more diagrams and attached them to Barker's whiteboard (Figure 5, Figure 6 and Table 1).

Figure 5 – Effective team blueprint

"I know this has been a huge amount of information today. However, it's important to get this point out early and at least introduce Table 1, which displays the decisions around the goal of effective teams (Ambler, Lines, 2019). *As we progress, we will see that the method I typically suggest is goal driven and always proving value, as Agent 13 says."*

Figure 6 - Goal, Decision, Options

Decision Points	Recommendation
Source of Team Members	Existing Product Team
Team Evolution Strategy	Team evolves itself
Size of Team	Small team of people
Team Structure	Single team
Member Skills	Generalizing specialists
Team Completeness	Whole team
Team Longevity	Stable team
Geographic Distribution	Co-located
Organisational Distribution	Multiple-division Full Time Equivalents (FTEs)
Time Zone Distribution	Same time zone
	Different time zones
Support the Team	Coaching, mentoring, training, Stakeholder access
Availability of Team Members	Dedicated
	Not Dedicated
Mindset for Team	Five DevOps Values

Table 1 – Forming effective teams' key decisions and some options

"How is 'a small team of people' defined?" Barker asked without looking up from his note taking.

"We believe that there is no one-size-fits-all. It depends on your context. You should experiment to find the team size that works for you," advised Agent 77.

"In my experience, I advocate the 6+-3 rule, plus the product owner and a Scrum Master; whereby the latter should become a revolving team role. Take some time to review the interesting Ringelman effect (Ringelmann, Maximilien, 2019),*"* Agent 13 supplemented.

"That is exactly the point about not being prescriptive, and the context counts is one of the key Disciplined Agile principles," said Agent 77. *"We choose our team size based on our situation, and this also fits perfectly with the lines of autonomy. The teams decide size because of the how and when, not the managers."*

Barker nodded hesitantly. *"Wow, that is a mind shift! Our managers always determine team size and decide when and how,"* he lamented. *"Well, actually, the leaders do that, and managers tow the line."*

"I'd like to define what is meant by team and team member, since referencing team size depends on context and being pragmatic. Teams can be defined in two groups – Primary and Supporting. The primary team involves those who are working directly on the product and solution each day, while the supporting team contains experts needed to support the primary team," Agent 77 quantified.

By now, Barker's eyes had begun to gloss over, and he had stopped taking notes. Rubbing his eyes, he remarked, *"I look forward to defining the roles, which will explain how teams range from two to fifty, but right now, my brain has reached maximum capacity. I think it may be best to let this information sink in before adding more.*

"Why don't you guys hang here while I assemble the team? I'll then fetch you when they are ready," Barker suggested as he walked towards the door of his office. *"We have our monthly IT meeting, so you're free for the next hour or so,"* he informed, saluting towards them as he left.

"Phew, what a day!" he thought at the same time as the AoCs.

Time for Change: We Want DevOps!

In the main auditorium, Barker addressed the key members that he handpicked for, what he called, his DevOps special team. These were people he trusted and believed understood Agile DevOps.

"Team, I know you have been doing Agile and, some of you, even DevOps. We want to improve on this because the Overlords and Maverick believe it will help us deliver and be more effective. I know, I know, it may sound like the flavour of the month, however, I

want you all to give your best and explore the DevOps mindset to help us improve our quality and performance.

"Honestly, our department costs are growing, quality is becoming more of a concern, and our response to rapidly changing business requirements is appearing to some as too slow. Any thoughts?"

Automaton, the perfectionist and operations guru who dabbles in infrastructure as code (IAC), raised his hand. "Simple, I have some new software, and we should simply automate everything."

Umpty, the cautious quality testing lead, timidly replied, "Ummm, err, the software sounds good, but I don't think we can automate everything."

Rabbit, a shy but smart developer, smiled and nodded while hiding behind her laptop, busily checking some code as usual.

Boundless, a new developer and UX upstart, ignoring both Umpty and Automaton, confidently exclaimed, "*All systems go! Where do we start?*"

Automaton rolled his eyes at Boundless.

Wiggle, the business analyst, looked off in the distance and asked, "*Aren't we already doing Agile or something? I mean, we are really busy with getting the new release out, should we not concentrate on that?*"

Knight, the shining armour operations lead and savvy infrastructure architect, assured, "*Don't worry. The release will be exactly on time. If necessary, although highly unlikely, I can work over the weekend to get the production servers ready.*"

"*I can help you, Knight,*" volunteered Redline, a developer and front-end expert. "*Oh, Barker? Could we get a coach or experts to help us?*"

"Perfect segue," thought Barker. *"Redline, that is a great idea. In fact, Maverick and I have invited three experts, called the Agents of Chaos, to mentor and guide us through this digital transformation. They are actually in my office, waiting to be introduced,"* he revealed.

The team was shocked at how gung-ho Barker seemed about this and the fact that he had already lined up experts to help. He typically did not subscribe to such things. Once Barker left the room to retrieve the AoCs, everyone began talking about DevOps and what they thought of it; everyone, that is, except Rabbit, who was busy making sure her code was flawless.

Barker returns to the room with the AoCs and introduces each of the agents to the team. The team showed interest in the agent's background and experience, which lead to interesting discussions.

***

Barker was relieved after the introductions had gone well; both the team and AoCs seemed impressed by one another. After the meeting, he escorted the AoCs to the lobby, thanked them for their time and bid them farewell for the day. He then went back to his office and ordered an electronic copy of the DevOps Handbook (Gene Kim, Patrick Debois, John Willis, and Jez Humble, 2016) and the Choose Your WoW (Ambler, Lines, 2019) for each member of his team.

After they downloaded the books, Barker thought, *"I am too pooped to read any more about this DevOps right now. I will read about it first thing in the morning."* He closed his laptop, shut off the lights and locked his office door on his way out. It had been a very productive, informative day, and he needed to decompress and recharge. He headed home filled with thoughts of a successful transformation.

The next day, Barker skimmed the two recent downloads. As expected, the books introduced enterprise awareness – the need to think about the whole organisation. Choose Your WoW had all the DAD goals and options in it, making it a great reference! The

DevOps Handbook was also easy to read and highlighted increasing profitability, elevating work culture, and exceeding productivity goals through DevOps practises.

Barker knew how important DevOps was to Maverick, and he began to grasp that DevOps was not just Agile, realising there was a lot more to learn! Therefore, he canceled his morning meetings and got down to reading more on it, pausing occasionally to daydream.

"I am going to be the Director of DevOps and impress Maverick and show those other managers why Maverick picked me to lead this! They will want to follow my example, or they will not be around much longer!" He relished his thoughts.

The more he read, the more Barker understood how involved it was. It was going to take some serious budget and several months to deliver. He kept seeing the word *journey*, which made him wonder to himself, *"How long are those AoCs around for? What are they charging us anyway? I had better speak with the procurement and contracts department to get some help to make DevOps happen. I'm also going to need some serious budget from Maverick to secure a DevOps project manager and bunch of new tools."*

Assess Your Uncharted DevOps: The River

Maverick called Barker into his office, filled with pictures of old IBM mainframes, which contrasted scenes out of a western canyon and abandoned towns. Maverick's interest in adventures into uncharted territories was clear.

"Barker, how did yesterday go? I hear you discussed a lot and introduced the AoCs to your DevOps team. What have you guys decided?"

Figure 7 – Agents of Chaos –Brent, David, Mathew, and Willy

Barker looked at Maverick then at each of the AoCs, who had arrived shortly before he was called in.

"Yesterday was great, and I really appreciate what I am learning so far. I do realise that people are a lot more important to success then I originally thought. I can thank the AoCs for that. However, I do believe in strict discipline and process, sir," he admitted.

Maverick chuckled. *"Well, I am glad that you can acknowledge those points and that the AoCs can help. We do not want folks stressed or freaked out because of change. Speaking of which, how much change do we need? Are we ready to begin our DevOps transformation? I mean, we have been doing Agile processes for a while now..."* Maverick stated, hoping to get a green light.

Barker nodded and poised to say, *"Oh yes, we are already doing this stuff,"* when Agent 13 masterfully interjected.

"We prefer to start with a foundation and initial insight. That is why we like to perform an assessment of the organisation's people, process, and products to reveal its current culture, leadership, teams, and, more importantly, the appetite for change. This is a very important first step towards being successful," Agent 13 explained.

Maverick absorbed this, suddenly remembering what happened the last time they tried putting Agile and a bunch of new processes into the IT teams; pure chaos and anarchy resulted! Why, some practically turned into rebels. It was almost a mutiny! Maverick shuddered at the memory of it all.

Agent 77, observing the body language assured, *"Many folks say they want to change but find it difficult to execute it. Enabling change is critical to the adoption of DevOps. We understand that, so we have developed a number of softer approaches to getting vital information."*

"Your teams need to feel safe and confident, so they can provide as candid and accurate feedback as possible," Agent 9 instructed.

Agent 13 nodded at his fellow AoCs and continued where Agent 9 left off.

"The assessment will highlight the areas that will transform naturally as well as those you will need to nurture thoughtfully. The assessment's benchmark of your DevOps mindset and performance is then compared to the rest of the industry. It is important to understand where you are doing well and, even more importantly, where investment will help take you to the next level.

"The DORA, SAFe DevOps radar, and Microsoft DevOps assessments are great starting points for the organisation and selected feature teams, assessing key areas, such as:

- *Culture*
- *Measurement*
- *Outcomes*
- *Process*
- *Technology and automation"*

"Additionally, thoughtful use of quick polls to collect data on the key performance indicators and culture complement the DevOps assessment. Always remember the quote by (Jack Welch, 2020), *'What gets measured gets done,'"* Agent 9 pointed out.

Agent 77, sensing that Barker and Maverick may gloss over this important part of their work, emphasised, *"The surveys need to be thoughtful, not just canned queries. We ask questions that will help derive data that can help us make good decisions and provide sound guidance."*

Maverick did not quite seem to grasp Agent 77's point, so he elaborated, *"Surveys can be subjective, which is why we have workshops, group discussions and face-to-face meetings. Of course, the assessments and surveys are anonymous, but we can find out which group or team the individual may be in to help that area, if you choose. We really want to encourage team members to be candid and unbiased, though."*

Maverick and Barker nodded as they began to understand what the AoCs were pushing.

"Assessments are not a once-off, fire-and-forget exercise. Repeat them, track trends, and share results transparently," Agent 13 reminded.

He then described the quick poll survey questions (AoC, 2020) found in the on the AoCs website. Highlighting some of the questions that Maverick and Barker may choose to use in their polls and surveys, he reviewed each, providing reasons for asking them to illustrate the benefit of this part of the process.

Agent 13 finished by stating, *"We should adapt the scale and evaluation of your response data to align with the **State of DevOps** (Puppet Labs, 2018) report. This allows you to baseline and compare your findings with the latest in the industry, consistently."*

"This makes sense," said Barker, once again enthused by the AoCs' information. *"I'm excited to get started!"*

For the next few days, Barker worked with the AoCs feverishly to create a custom set of questions and polls. Barker introduced the AoCs to the Data Science Department, which oversees corporate questionnaires. The AoCs, with input from Barker and the Data Science team, completed a digital survey that they then distributed to select teams within the IT department to test its effectiveness before distributing it to the rest of the teams. This allowed them to review the data and tweak the questions to ensure sure they received real answers and people were not "gaming the system".

The questions and polls were based on Microsoft's DevOps Self-assessment (Microsoft, 2020) and experienced questions the AoCs used previously to derive data aligned with the State of DevOps Report (Puppet, CircleCI and Splunk, 2019).

The AoCs actively engaged with each team, meeting both 1:1 and in groups, and provided a set of definitions referenceable on the IT departments Wiki. They also explained the purpose of the assessments and responded to questions and concerns from the team members. The AoCs reinforced the importance of everyone understanding the purpose of the assessment and how the findings would be used to track the organisation's health to support the digital transformation journey.

 A frequent reminder not to link assessment findings to individuals or their career planning or evaluations was repeated consistently by the AoCs at each meeting. They wanted to make sure the assessments did not become finger pointing exercises where no friends are gained!

After several days, the data from the assessment survey was analyzed and used to create a report that could be part of a DevOps "health and adoption dashboard," which the AoCs reviewed with Maverick before taking it to Barker.

The results showed that there were some individuals who were more familiar with and willing to advocate, support and test the DevOps mindset than others. Maverick, having had time to digest the data, began the meeting.

"I believe it is important for us not to run too far or fast with the output from this report. Rather, we must take a pragmatic step-by-step approach. In other words, let us focus on the step, not the staircase."

Agent 13 nodded at this suggestion.

"This opportunity should identify one or two teams that can become a lighthouse for the rest of the organisation, helping us promote a DevOps mindset and enable others to transform," he appended.

Barker looked disappointed after digesting the information and comments. His department had scored a low response rate. Those that had actually responded showed a general lack of understanding in DevOps.

"I agree with both of you about how to use this data," he assured. *"But I am, however, slightly concerned about the lack-luster survey response rate,"* he admitted.

Agent 13 frowned.

"Do not worry. If you get more than a 20% response, you are doing exceptionally well. Future assessments will be much easier once your teams have embraced and realised the value of continuous feedback and learning," he said, consoling Barker's concerns.

"OK," Barker perked up. *"I will continue to monitor the response rate and peek into the data to get an early sense of emerging results and patterns."*

The discussion continued until Maverick felt satisfied that he could move forward with a better understanding of where his department was on the DevOps scale.

"Thanks, everyone. Remember that we are going to share the important and pivotal information from these results once we have polished the presentation," he informed, knowing he needed some time to finalize its display.

The group parted ways and prepared to begin their journey.

Map Your Digital Transformation Journey

A month later at the monthly IT meeting, everyone eagerly awaited insight into the assessment results. Maverick and Barker stood in front, while the AoCs sat with the rest of the IT department, which packed the auditorium. Barker looked a bit nervous, feverishly clicking through the presentation.

*"The **State of DevOps Report**, which we shared with all of you some time ago, highlights that teams developing and delivering their solutions quickly are able to experiment, reflect, and pivot as necessary to continuously delight their customers."* He clicked to the next slide.

"As you all know, we recently conducted two assessments; one after we announced the need for change and another after we engaged in vibrant discussions of our people, process, and products." The next slide appeared on the screen.

"So, I'm sure you're all wondering what we found. Do we, as an organisation, have an appetite for change? How, if at all, has your feedback changed?" He placed the projection clicker on the podium and gestured towards the side of the stage.

"Please welcome our IT CIO, Maverick, who will share the findings and some conclusions discussed with the Overlords. Sir, the stage is all yours!"

Maverick walked onto the stage, smiling and waving to the large group. He was in his element.

"Team, I want to take this opportunity to thank everyone for providing candid and actionable feedback, and being committed to reflect, continuously innovate, and improve our people, process and products. Now, let us unpack the assessment results."

At this, Agent 9 suddenly leaned over to Agent 77 with a puzzled look and asked, *"Why is Maverick presenting the results and not Barker?"*

"Maverick wants to show that the leadership is fully committed to the digital transformation. He wants to inspire everyone!" replied Agent 77.

The AoCs scanned the auditorium. For the first time, everyone seemed very engaged; Rabbit was not even hiding behind her laptop as Maverick continued.

"Your feedback offers an insight into opportunities for continuous improvement.

"As shown in Figure 8, we enjoyed a significant increase in feedback in the second survey we conducted. Thank you for your interest in and appetite for our digital transformation."

Figure 8 – Six teams that took part in the assessment

Maverick's excitement was clear in is voice as he continued to unpack these important key findings.

- **"Shifting testing and security LEFT with continuous integration** will raise our quality bar and complement the practise of continuous delivery. Combined with fast feedback, reflection and remediation, our teams can mature to deploy on-demand.

- **"We all need to understand what the DevOps entails,** why our organisation is investing in the digital transformation, and how we can all take responsibility for our engineering system and business features from start to finish.

- **"Proactive monitoring and tracking key performance indicators (KPI) to unearth quality and value is challenging** but essential to finding waste, opportunity for improvement, and the ability to delight users."

Maverick stopped for a moment and took a sip of water, looking out at his teams that were hanging on his every word. He liked to intentionally introduce a long pause to allow for drama, but it also gave everyone in the room a chance to digest the storm of information.

Maverick raised his voice slightly to resume.

"At the core are people ... every one of you! You are unique and the key. The processes, technology, product and our size make much less difference! You differentiate us from other organisations!"

Everyone in the auditorium clapped and cheered. Maverick then lowered his voice.

"If you have read Dan Pink's book or watched his video about what motivates us, you will appreciate that autonomous teams, driven by purpose and mastery, should strive to be in a performance-oriented band." He pointed to the slide projected high on the 80-foot screen. *"As shown in* Figure 9, *we are hovering between a performance and rule-oriented team culture."*

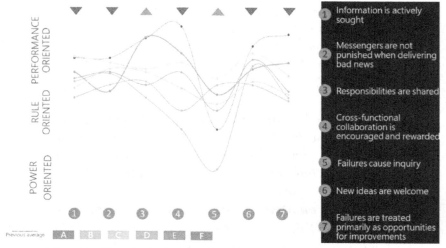

Figure 9 – Organisation's culture pivots between rule and performance orientated

Maverick forced a long period of silence, making eye contact with everyone. *"The next slide (Figure 10) is worrying."*

The clapping and cheering came to an abrupt end.

"Evidently, only one team would recommend our organisation to their friends as a place to work. I take responsibility and will get to the bottom of this."

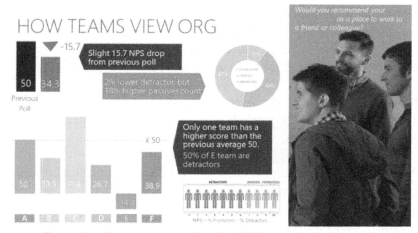

Figure 10 – Teams are not comfortable with the organisation's transformation

Maverick took another sip of water, nodding to the AoCs in agreement and intentionally pausing again to invite questions. When none surfaced, he moved on.

"Figure 11 highlights four areas where the views of our leadership vary significantly from our engineering self-assessments.

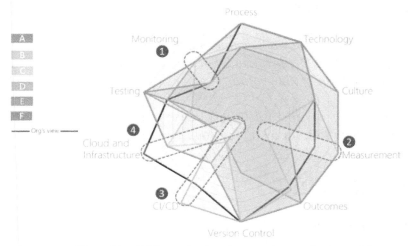

Figure 11 – Difference in views between the organisation and its teams

"Monitoring is more positive from the teams than the organisation. Measurement of value, user and server performance seems to be

viewed very differently between the two. There is also significant contrast with continuous integration and delivery pipelines, as well as with cloud and infrastructure, all having a more conservative view from the teams. These are areas of opportunity!"

At this point Maverick required help explaining the output and figures, so he invited Agent 13, who was already aware of this need, onto the stage.

"Agent 13, can you elaborate on why continuous monitoring and observation are important?"

"Certainly! By continuously tracking key performance indicators (KPI) and striving to achieve better outcomes, we can introduce value, get feedback, and mitigate issues more quickly.

"This means that end-users are delighted and engineers motivated. It is a WIN-WIN!" exclaimed Agent 13, fiddling with his microphone.

KPI to increase

*"**Deployment Frequency** determines how many deployments are made in production. Deployments that are more frequent allow earlier introduction of new value.*

"Let us look at three other KPIs, which we must decrease," he said, signaling to Maverick for a slide change.

KPIs to decrease

*"**Change Failure Rate** is the relationship between our changes and outages in production. More successful changes cut rework and allow us to focus on new value."* He cued the next slide.

*"**Lead Time for Change** is our average time between receiving a feature request and deploying it to production. Shorter lead times enable faster feedback and the ability for us to respond to outages more effectively.*

"Lastly," he continued, pausing for the next slide. *"My favourite: **Mean Time to Recover/Repair (MTTR)!** This is the average time we need to repair a failed part, device, or feature. Faster time to mitigate failures gives our users higher availability. The lower the better!"*

Maverick was delighted that the AoCs were talking about "us" and instilling a sense of teamwork between permanent and part-time staff, as well as their consultants. He often reminded his transformation critics that there is no 'I' in 'them', 'us' or 'team'.

"Agent 13, allow me to expand on MTTR with an example," Maverick interjected. *"Say you phone your service provider to report a problem with your device, and you're placed on hold, listening to soul quenching jingles and constant reminders that your call is important.*

"Does this really feel make you, the customer, feel important? Then, after holding for half an hour, you're bounced between departments, only to end up back on hold. This is a horrid MTTR experience.

"Figure 12 illustrates that we need to do better in this area!" Maverick raised his eyebrows at the audience, while he waited for the importance of this to sink in.

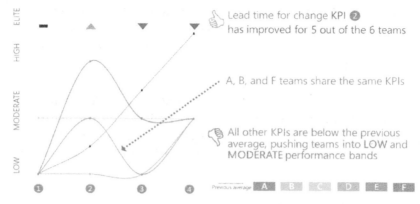

Lead time for change KPI ② has improved for 5 out of the 6 teams

A, B, and F teams share the same KPIs

All other KPIs are below the previous average, pushing teams into LOW and MODERATE performance bands

Figure 12 – The four key performance indicators (KPI) to embrace

"This reminds me of a Dynamic Duo," Agent 13 said. *"Remember not to track and assess your key performance indicators in isolation. For example, a high deployment frequency and a high change failure rate is a smell,"* he cautioned.

After a moment, Maverick switched off the projector, saying, *"That's it for a presentation. Let's get the rest of the AoCs up here and find out what's next!"*

Agents 9 and 77 joined Agent 13, Maverick and Barker on stage. Agent 14 had preferred to remain at the Docks (the nickname of their workspace).

"As we briefly discussed during our report out and review a while ago, this presentation has given your Agile development teams the opportunity to understand how you compare with the organisation and rest of the industry," Agent 13 summarised. *"Now, it is important to reflect, pivot, and focus on where we can improve.*

"The other AoCs and I feel that the takeaways are:
- *Firstly, we want delighted customers and stakeholders.*
- *Secondly, we should work together to progress to high-performing and, eventually, elite teams.*

"Keep in mind that the DevOps Mindset is a journey with a destination you are unlikely to ever reach. It is about continuous improvement!"

 Consider these checklists and ideas down the road: Expand your culture to embrace a DevOps mindset (AoC, 2020), Streamline your processes (AoC, 2020), and Improve the technical practises (AoC, 2020).

Maverick and Barker nodded to each other in agreement.

"Anything else, Agents?" Maverick asked.

"Actually, Maverick," Agent 9 replied. *"Looking at Figure 13, there seems to be a disconnect between the assessment of our technical practises and the feedback from our teams. ... no?"*

Figure 13 – How painful are the deployments?

Maverick re-read the results.

"Great observation, Agent 9! Some of the teams are a shadow team within one of our customers, bound to their processes and products when it comes to releasing new features," Maverick explained.

"It is important to extend your digital transformation boundary to include your customer," Agent 9 replied. *"They are part of the stakeholders that need to understand your vision, and the impact and value to their business. Break down the barriers!"*

 Treat your users as invaluable knowledge workers or **assets,** not as resources to command and move around like sheep in a field! **Lead**, not manage!

"OK, we will explore ways to share our Agile DevOps transformation journey, learnings, and challenges with our customers and the broader community as you suggested. Perhaps through the community of practise or CoP?" Maverick looked for confirmation from the AoCs.

"May I make one small comment?" Agent 13 asked with a smile.

"Of course."

Turning to the audience, Agent 13 said, *"Please help us and do yourselves a favour by referring to your transformation journey as Agile **and/or** DevOps, not Agile DevOps! The clarification is important."*

No one noticed Barker turn red as he made a mental note to avoid making that mistake again.

Please! Stop calling it Agile DevOps!

Agile is **not** an adjective of DevOps! Agile is a way of working, a toolkit, framework or methodology made popular by the Agile Manifesto, which was created by software developers with software development in mind. Lean and Agile can be used in, what is now referred to as, Business Agility, which expands on the Agile Manifesto (agilemanifesto.org). DevOps is a mindset that is **not** dependent on Agile. However, teams with an Agile mindset or using Agile techniques are more likely to benefit when extending Agile to include the DevOps mindset. Consider expanding Agile from your development teams to include operations and the rest of IT. The data connection between DevOps and Agile is clearly shown in reports, such as the *State of the Union Report* right through 2019.

Excitement was in the air of the audience as Maverick wrapped-up the presentation.

"The organisation has completed step one and officially embarked on its exciting digital transformation journey of continuous innovation with no destination. Let the fun begin!" Maverick triumphantly declared.

"I want us to become a performance-oriented organisation. I see no reason, based on our results, that we cannot all approach the upper band when we process our next assessment." He looked to the AoCs for affirmation.

"Say, in a month or so?" Barker offered instead.

The AoCs gave an approving nod, and the assembly adjourned.

After the presentation, Maverick beamed and Barker glowed. Many of the team members had approached them and the AoCs to express their gratitude for the significant effort put towards transformation and appreciation for being included in the surveys and interviews.

As the AoCs, Barker and Maverick left together, Agent 77 asked for a quiet word alone with Maverick, who stepped aside and found a private corner to chat.

"What did you think of the presentation?" Maverick asked him, hoping for positive feedback.

"I think you did a great job and really fired everyone up. The other AoCs and I can see that the whole IT organisation is energised and engaged by your sponsorship and support through this change."

Maverick smiled. *"Thank you, and I appreciate of your hard work, however, I feel you are holding something back,"* Maverick prodded.

"With all due respect, I would like to raise one point that I think will help us very much," Agent 77 admitted, waiting for, and receiving, permission to continue. *"There is a need to allow the teams to feel empowered to make decisions on how they work. This gives them the ability to take risks while innovating or experimenting. Receiving support from management to accept failures often and as an opportunity to learn makes them more willing to take those necessary risks."*

Maverick thought seriously about what Agent 77 said. The two remained quiet for a moment, contemplating how to achieve it.

"On the other hand, your teams must also take responsibility and be ready, as if on-call, to foster personal interest to action and a value first mindset," Agent 77 concluded.

Maverick understood and agreed with this point and thanked him for his candor. He then made a point to remember to share this additional insight with Barker.

"Let's all grab a drink at the pub next door where you can help me articulate that to Barker," he suggested.

"You bet!" Agent 77 replied. *"Music to my ears!"*

Final Thoughts and Next Steps

It is clear from the net promoter scores that transformation of the culture is the biggest challenge. Leadership must continue to promote a climate of continuous learning, experimentation, and transparency. Also, continuing to share the DevOps vision, so teams understand **why** and **how** they will be affected and the importance of taking responsibility for the **how** and **when** of creating and owning their features is crucial to success.

The next step should be reviewing how to align business capabilities with an effective technical and organisational architecture. Teams should not exceed the cognitive limit of a "2 pizza" collaborative unit. Crack open engineering and business processes, map **value streams**, define a **common language**, and bridge the gap between business, engineering, and customers. **Destroy the silos**!

Kanban and other visualisation techniques help organisations track and visualize the flow of **business value** from ideation to delivery, highlight areas of waste and opportunity, and bring business, engineering, and other stakeholders closer together.

Checkout the Creating effective teams with a DevOps mindset (AoC, 2020).

DevOps Mindset Value 1 Goal Reached

 Well done, we have reached our first goal: **Measure performance across the organisation** not just a line of business.

From the early discussions with Maverick, the AoC established business values and change that align with the businesses, goals. An important lesson for the folks in IT because effective teams are across the organisation, not just IT! Thus, transformation programs are a change to the whole systems rather than a single component. When we change a part (component), such as a team in IT we measure this, we improve this, and we map our digital transformation so we can see the effect of our changes and improvements as individual, team and across the organisation. The first core value is a significant mind shift because we measure what matters, and we are looking beyond our team!

Afternoon Huddle aka "The Dock"

Before heading to the pub, Barker and Maverick caught up on their emails and other action items that had filtered in throughout the day while the AoCs went back to the Docks to regroup and assess the progress to date. There, hard at work, sat Agent 14, drawing up more templates and diagrams to use in facilitating the transformation. Although usually behind the scenes, Agent 14 was a very talented artist who contributed much value to the AoCs' ability to guide organisations along in their journeys.

The AoCs discussed Big Corp's progression, bringing Agent 14 up to speed as they did every afternoon.

Using metaphors in line with sailing, like rocks, waves or sharks, for unexpected obstacles or challenges, they tried to make sure they were aware of any turbulence in the waters ahead.

"Agent 77, how did your chat with Maverick go? What was his take on the presentation? Do you see any potential hazards?"

Before Agent 77 could answer, Agent 13 jumped in with his concerns.

"I fear that two large and dangerous sharks, lurking in the water, may be the misalignment of expectations within leadership and the teams' lack of autonomy. I worry that Maverick views DevOps as a silver harpoon and is placing immensely high expectations and difficult deadlines on the team, which will cause them to buckle under the pressure."

"I totally agree, Agent 13," affirmed Agent 9. *"I am a firm believer that organisation change initiatives, like an Agile or DevOps transformation, should be top-down with a management team that understands what Agile and DevOps can and cannot deliver."* The others nodded in agreement. *"Anything short of that is setting the organisation up for failure just like in the Waterfall days where expectations could not be managed correctly."*

"Precisely," stated Agent 77. *"And, as usual, we have uncovered many challenges and opportunities already! I am glad that we helped establish a baseline of what DevOps is and what it is not. That was so important."* He grabbed an itinerary template created by Agent 14 to chart the next leg of their route. *"The next step is reeling in the mindset so that pragmatism, context and choice are all clear,"* he continued, writing as he spoke. *"We need to help Maverick and Barker understand the goals of DevOps that align to their corporate goals, and define the scope, so we can help launch their DevOps program successfully!"*

Boat Inspection

Lost at Sea – No Clarity on WHAT or WHY

One day, Agent 77 decided to visit another team he had not coached before, observing one of their daily stand-up ceremonies, also known as a Scrum. Agent 77 was not invited to this stand-up, so he followed his own advice to remain silent and simply observe.

Entering the team's area, he got the eerie sense that the project had no chance of success. After the Scrum, and when the opportunity arose, he decided to ask a few questions while the team were deliberating on what exactly they were building.

"Excuse me, Team, but what is the business or architectural vision for why we are we doing this project, and how does it align with the organisation's visions, goals, and technical governance?"

Unfortunately, and rather expectedly, no one was clear on **WHAT** the exact objective was, **WHY** their project was important, or **WHERE** they were heading. In fact, the vision was so unclear that most team members had stopped believing that project success was even attainable. Everyone looked exhausted and remained silent.

"This is like wandering around a ghost ship filled with skeletons and smelly, dead fish," thought Agent 77, discouraged by the scene.

It was clear that the team's harpoon project was fast becoming destructive to the organisation, demoralizing the team and stakeholders. No one was energised, and stakeholders were unlikely to tolerate the inflated cost to value ratio for much longer – it was time to readjust!

Agent 77 decided to take the wheel and steer the ship back on course. He could see several milestones in their backlog that were either missing or being overlooked.

"Team, if I may, I would like to share some observations," he said, looking around the room at hopeful faces. *"First, I do not physically see the project vision. Barker, you need to own your **vision** and share it with your team by displaying it in the workspace! What happened to the business and architecture vision statements?"*

Barker's face reddened.

"Umm, well..." he stuttered as he searched for an explanation. Looking at the space on the whiteboard that had since been erased, he contended, *"I explained my understanding of the vision and the plan to achieve it. I even wrote it on the whiteboard, like you advised! It was meant to remain there until we delivered."*

"You are also supposed to document as you go," Agent 77 reminded him.
"Clearly, we missed that as well," Barker admitted. *"I shall ensure we catch these important statements in the future."*

Barker looked embarrassed but also determined to correct these oversights.

"Good," lauded Agent 77. *"Be sure to use **business** that is **engineering-friendly** and **language** that is **consistent** in your stories and documentation."*

"We are trying," Barker assured him. *"But it is not as easy as I thought it would be to remember all the terminology."*

Agent 77 was not surprised to hear this as this is a common issue in any organisational culture change.

"Create a clear list of definitions to avoid ambiguity. Try regularly referring to IT and enterprise architecture standards to align everyone with the organisation's technical governance!" Agent 77 suggested.

Barker was already aware that he owned the vision, but this explained why. The vision was the lighthouse and he the lighthouse keeper! He needed to clearly articulate and share the vision and goals with the team, using inspiring and consistent communication.

He knew that, once the team understood WHAT they needed to achieve and WHY, they could plan HOW and WHEN they would deliver the features that were aligned with the portfolio, value stream, and overall technical governance.

 Leaders must inspire the team, accept failures as an opportunity for continuous improvement, and recognise and celebrate success to rejuvenate the team's passion. Ghost ships are scary. However, once you repair the team's area and remove the dead fish, they typically turn into sublime dream liners.

"If you're going through hell, keep going." – Winston Churchill

Act 2

PEOPLE - A Turbulent Journey

Another Morning Chat

Agent 13 mulled over a question about team sizes while patiently waiting for Agent 77 to return from a DevOps Meetup at another corporation. The topic of team size seemed to be causing uncertainty, even outside Big Corp. People were unsure what the team sizes should be. Agent 13 had recently launched an online community poll, asking folks in the DevOps Meetup what their experience has been with this concept. The results varied, and he looked forward to Agent 77's input.

"Oh good, you're back!" he said, taking the coffee Agent 77 offered him. *"The community polls have confirmed that 6+-3 and 7+-2 are the popular team sizes for Lean teams with a DevOps mindset."* He skipped the pleasantries and got straight to the point. *"Personally, I favour the 6+-3 guidelines, bolstered with other cross-functional, partially allocated but fully committed roles for the development team. What is your thought on the ideal team size?"*

Agent 77 smiled, delighted with his colleague's enthusiasm.

"Well, evidence and experience suggest smaller teams usually are pretty effective. A small team should not hamper scaling because there can be sub-teams or feature teams (Scrum of scrums-esque), meaning that these smaller teams are typically in the range of 2-15 people. Keep in mind that we should not be prescriptive, and there are trade-offs with any choice we make. We are continually evolving our team's "way of working," discovering our team size's sweet spot for each product over time. Of course, this will vary, depending the decision of each team."

Agent 13 was glad he had consulted Agent 77.

"So, no more than 15 members, or do you mean that we let the team decide what the right size is and try not to constrain them by dictating a certain size?" he asked.

"Exactly the latter. The members and situation may result in the DevOps delivery team varying in size. Remember, we are talking about one team that is delivering, not an entire IT department that

should be actively pursuing the DevOps mindset," Agent 77 reiterated.

Agents 13 and 77 reviewed the results shown in Figure 14.

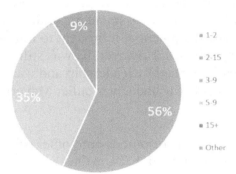

Figure 14 – Community Poll: Team Size

The typical team size was around 3-9 engineers, but they could see that, as with so many things in the industry, there was no one-size-fits-all. Both Agents of Chaos were familiar with Cynefin, a conceptual framework used to better understand your culture and business operations. In fact, all the AoCs believe that it is important to "probe, sense, and respond", as outlined in the Cynefin Sensemaking model (Boone, 2007) for complex models.

Poking the hornets' nest means that you should **think seriously not to grow your teams beyond the "two pizza" size!**

Just like with requirements, features, and stories, refactor teams into smaller, productive, and passionate **synchronised** teams!

Why Not Just Buy and Install DevOps?

The AoCs returned to their Big Corp work area, the Dock, to catch up on emails and such. They shared temporary desks, in an open area, surrounded by whiteboards, quick reference posters, and sticky notes. They also used a flat screen TV to show "rolling" information and dashboards to anyone as they walked by.

Barker strolled into the Dock, whistling. After several weeks of working with AoCs and the assessment, he understood DevOps much better and saw the potential it brought to improving performance and processes. However, he was still confused by some of the new terminology used by leadership and was not fully convinced that DevOps was the silver bullet Maverick made it out to be.

Thus, Barker allocated his resources onto other priorities to keep the ship running. He still doubted that DevOps was more than the latest fad. The AoCs, sensing a disturbance in the water, noticed other managers viewing DevOps similarly as well. They knew they needed to address this perspective in addition to Barker's reluctance to commit his staff full-time to the DevOps program, citing a lack of resources.

Agent 77 planned to approach this dilemma carefully. Barker sat down and was watching the ticker on the TV screen update him on the status of iterations when Agent 77 cleared his throat.

"Barker, I'll get straight to the point," he said. *"I understand resources are hard to come by, and you have many changing priorities. Continuing our travel by boat analogy, if we were to embark on a cross-Atlantic journey, what type of boat would you use? Would you perform small tests and experiments to determine the right size, strength, power and capability of the boat while training the whole crew? Would you have everyone practise safety drills, testing the equipment and procedures, to ensure the boat was sound and sailors ready to travel?"*

"Hmm, well, I suppose I would start with a small, nimble boat, but I fail to see the point in bringing safety equipment or using the whole team during the testing phase," he stated. *"If the weather reports look good, the extra equipment would simply add weight, cause unnecessary costs, increase complexity and waste valuable space."*

Agent 13 watched Barker's body language and sensed that he was not aligned with many of the points Agent 77 was raising.

"Barker, your DevOps journey should be based on an empirical process control and a quest to continuously streamline, inspect, and adapt. You should have complete transparency of failures and success. However, your team needs to be safe, so they feel supported and willing to keep validating, innovating and improving. We AoCs believe that DevOps is fundamentally the mindset of continuously adding value to the organisation as quickly as possible for the engineering system and your customer. It is not something you can do half-heartedly or overnight," Agent 77 urged.

"In other words," Agent 13 interjected. *"You cannot make this unknown journey, using assumptions based on short-term weather predictions or the first version of the boat, be it small or large!"*

Everyone realised that Barker was looking for a quick fix; a product that provided an out-of-the-box, integrated and collaborative DevOps engineering system. He wanted a ready to go, ready to deploy approach, based on his current operations and resources, including scheduling, release planning, help desk, knowledge and the rest of how IT was currently working.

Barker shook his head. *"We do not have the luxury of unlimited time to pursue an unknown DevOps destination. Why can we not simply automate or make pipelines, using a product to inject DevOps into our organisation to transform and enable our Agile development teams?"* he asked in frustration.

Agent 13 knew it was time to now bring up the 80/15/5 rule. *"Successful organisations, especially those that effectively bring value to delighted customers, typically have a ratio of 5% about PRODUCT, 15% about PROCESS, and 80% about PEOPLE. Because people are so important, that is where you must start and focus. PEOPLE!"* Agent 13 said, trying to maintain control of his own rising frustrations.

"Remember, DevOps is not a silver bullet or something you can just buy and install. DevOps is something you do," Agent 9 added, calmly.

Barker grew more impatient with the process after listening to the AoCs and, unnecessarily, feared more feedback from them. He decided to search on the internet for *"DevOps + The Agents of Chaos"* to see what the results were. Presented with several articles they had authored, he downloaded the DevOps Transformation Guide (AoC, 2019) and Analysing the DNA of DevOps (AoC, 2018) and began reading.

After he finished, Barker questioned, *"Agents, why do you believe that we would find traces of Waterfall, Lean Thinking, Agile, Scrum, Kanban, and other genetic material in samples of teams under the microscope, as shown in Figure 15?"*

Figure 15 - DevOps DNA Helix

Agents 77 and 9 explained that DevOps inherits from a variety of proven and evolving frameworks. If you are comfortable with Lean Thinking and Agile, you get the full benefits of DevOps. However, if you are from a Waterfall environment, you can still benefit from a DevOps mindset.

The AoCs continued to demonstrate these concepts from the article. They pointed out the traces of Waterfall used for developing detailed and predictable scope, Lean for cutting waste, and Agile for promoting increments of shippable code. The genetic strands that define when and how to ship the code is where DevOps excels in the DNA analysis.

The AoCs cited a recently conducted a community poll they created to validate their assumptions. As shown in Figure 16, the poll confirmed their belief that DevOps is based on a variety of other proven genetics.

In engineering terms:
- *DevOps != Agile != Lean Thinking != Waterfall*
- *DevOps ⊂ Agile ⊂ Lean Thinking ⊂ Waterfall*

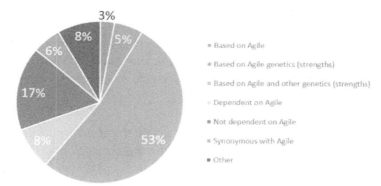

Figure 16 - Community Poll: DevOps DNA

Understanding the Boat Needed

The AoCs continued to share their learnings and recommendations with Barker, who took arduous notes. He frowned at the percentages that Agent 13 wrote next to products, process, and people on the whiteboard in bold letters.

5%
About PRODUCTS

15%
About PROCESS

80%
About PEOPLE

Barker looked up and thought for a moment, then said *"I know where you are going, Agents; people, people, people. I get it; however, people are so unpredictable, which is why I prefer using technology first! Maverick told me about a product he saw at a recent executive briefing named Acme Super DevOps. Why don't we just buy that solution, install it, and train our team? We can get the people to learn the product and then we can practise DevOps right away!"*

Agent 13 smiled but said, *"Although an excellent product, it only represents only up to 5% of your digital transformation.*

"Say you buy the best boat available on the market (product) with artificial intelligence and automation. You may have a great boat, but without operating and emergency procedures (process), and a good captain and crew (people) with the right commitment, skills, and mindset, you are sure to have a major accident that was preventable."

Barker recalled, *"Yes, that is what Agent 77 explained a few minutes ago."*

"Now, with people are the processes. Boats must follow rules and regulations, so effective people shall ensure the processes are

developed to meet or exceed the rules and regulations. *Further, to have the best services for your customers, you would add more value by improving your processes and adding products like technology to win more customers and delight them,"* Agent 13 expanded. He could see Barker absorbing the information.

"DevOps is more about what the people contribute (commitment, skills, knowledge) and the processes put in place than it is about the product. It is a mindset, and there are no unicorns!" finished Agent 13.

Barker nodded again and looked at Agent 9, who said, *"To start your transformation off correctly, we need to identify a team to lead it and become an inspiring lighthouse for the rest of your organisation. At the core of the transformation is people's buy-in to DevOps. It is important they understand how they will be impacted and take responsibility for their part in it."*

Barker winced. He knew the AoCs made sense.

"Look, I get it," he said, trying not to sound impatient. *"But I am getting major pushback from the business department that believes DevOps is just more IT & technical engineering jargon."*

Agent 9 scoffed, *"Understandable and a common misconception. DevOps is not limited to development and operations, despite its very name excluding other stakeholders. A key to the transformation is breaking down all barriers, walls, and silos within your organisation and bringing together all stakeholders, including development, data services, operations, security, and business."*

Agent 77 drew a high-level flow of feedback between DevOps teams, which clearly identified how DevOps connected to the whole enterprise.

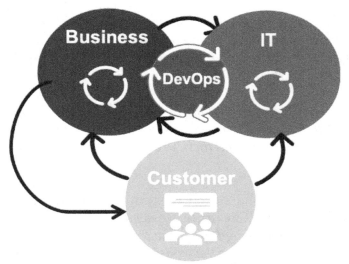

DevOps is connected across your enterprise
and beyond

Figure 17 - high-level flow of feedback between DevOps teams

"Go back to our boat analogy. We need a captain that accepts failures in a safe environment, as a normal opportunity to learn and improve. The threat of walking the plank is neither motivational, nor a means to continuous innovation," he explained. *"If we want the crew's culture to be one of learning, innovation and cross-functional collaboration, they need to be encouraged to give and receive feedback.*

"Your teams and individual members should be empowered with responsibility, focused on value. Instill a sense of responsibility and accountability to their team and organisation. They should be encouraged to try new things, see it works and fail early and safely by not being penalised if the original expectations are not being realised," he continued.

Barker paid close attention, linking his notes together.

"In other words," Barker began. *"Train them to sail the boat in any situation such as a storm?"* he asked.

"Absolutely!" Agent 77 confirmed. *"That way, if we are hit by a typhoon, every crew member – from the engineer maintaining the engine compartments to the sailor serving hot coffee in the bridge – is capable of, and empowered and motivated to actively support safe navigation of the boat through the storm to its destination."*

Although the DevOps transformation journey was only into its second month, Barker feverishly scribbled into a new, third journal, already filled with notes, recommendations, revelations, and learnings. Along the way, he had been compiling a small treasure chest of knowledge.

Barker's head was overflowing with all that was there to take in, and he still wanted to read more of what the AoCs had written. After thanking the AoCs for their time, he went to the cafeteria to get a hot drink and sit down to review a presentation Agent 13 had delivered called, Lessons Learned by an Agent of Chaos from DevOps Transformations (Agent 13, 2019).

Concerned that the transformation would fail, Barker set out to uncover why IT and, especially, operations were reluctant to make changes that the DevOps mindset calls out. He wondered why development teams reverted to their old ways of working in silos or, worse yet, by-passed operations entirely, creating a DevOps "special team with special rules".

He hoped that, after a short time, things would not go right back to how they were at the beginning. He sipped his coffee and studied. Agent 13's presentation provided a lot of information he needed to unpack, so after he finished with his coffee and reading material, Barker returned to the Dock to pick the AoCs' brains some more.

After informing them on his recent research, he asked several questions for more clarity.

*"Agent 13, in your **Lessons Learned by an Agent of Chaos from DevOps Transformations** presentation, you argued that DevOps in IT has been impaired by slow adoption of embracing innovation and experimentation. You also mention that software development teams*

*are typically keen to embrace agility and Lean concepts, such as
Lean management and Lean development, as they like continuous
delivery whereas operation teams resist. Could you explain that a
little more?"*

Agent 13 thought back to his presentation at the DevSecOps
conference in May 2019.

*"Sure. Over the past decade, development teams used the adoption
opportunities to pursue those practises and techniques, but
operation teams were not as privileged. Few innovations have been
made to the Information Technology Infrastructure Library (ITIL),
and the focus remains on quality (development) because releases are
often still viewed as bigger, less frequent super-tankers,"* Agent 13
expanded, waiting for Barker to prompt for more detail.

Barker looked concerned, admitting, *"We use ITIL. Is that a
problem?"*

Agent 77 shook his head. *"Absolutely not!"* he exclaimed, hoping
Agent 13 would not mind his interruption. *"Let's dissect the reasons
operations resists DevOps. First, developers are adding features and
improving their product while operations improves the services to
ensure the product meets the expectations of the business and users
of the product. Unnecessarily, this can cause friction between the
departments and teams when, in fact, the goals and principles of
ITIL are complementary and similar."* He grabbed a marker and
began writing on a whiteboard.

"For example, ITIL has principles, such as:
- *Focus on value*
- *Design for experience*
- *Start where you are*
- *Work holistically*
- *Progress iteratively*
- *Observe directly*
- *Be transparent*
- *Collaborate*
- *Keep it simple*

"Do these ITIL principles sound similar to Lean, Continuous Delivery, Innovation, self-organisation, automation and other points the AoCs have shared with you and Maverick?" Agent 77 asked, pointing to the list he had just written out.

Barker nodded, getting more excited.

"Okay, so we may have issues to overcome with our operations team. However, I am interested in more details on what opportunities there are for the development teams," Barker directed.

Agent 13 took his laptop over to Barker to show him the DevOps Wiki page on Terminology and Definitions he was updating. Scrolling through, he said, *"Actually, I am adding these terms in now.*

- ***Lean management*** *teams create a production-first observation and feedback loop, lightweight change approvals based on trust and empowerment, and visual cues to display the state of the transformation.*

- ***Lean development*** *encourages the team to experiment, learn, and influence. They continuously see, gather, and respond to production feedback. Managing work-in-progress (WIP) limits, working in small batches (short iterations), and adding visual cues for the flow of work and value is key to their success.*

- ***Continuous delivery*** *promotes built-in quality, continuous improvement and all-in responsibility, working in small batches and using computers to automate repetitive and automatable tasks."*

Barker was happy to have the terms clearly defined. He noticed the AoCs moving their work in progress for review on the Kanban board, displayed on a large TV screen in the Dock. He remembered he could look at the Kanban board anytime from any device and see an exact state of the nation.

"Could this be automated better," he wondered. Barker refocused, *"What about automation? Automaton says it is the secret key to DevOps."*

"Automation is important and part of the ITIL framework as well," Agent 77 said, looking over at Agents 13 and 9.

Agent 13 agreed with caution, *"It is true that automation is important, but you should focus on automating everything automatable, not everything period!"*

"Automation allows the team to focus on delivering value, however not everyone feels that you can automate everything!" Agent 9 added, pointing to the summary page on the DevOps Wiki where internal and community polls from the DevOps local Community of Practises (CoPs) that the AoCs were actively involved with were published. *"We collected this data over a number of months, both from your assessment and community polls. The results are very similar, and we see that only a quarter of in these polls believe that automating everything is the answer (Figure 18)."*

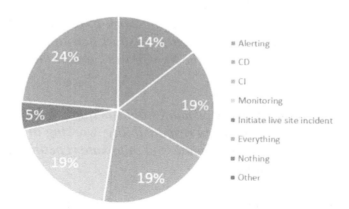

Figure 18 - Community poll: To automate or not to automate

Barker was thrilled that the AoCs provided more evidence, correlating and comparing data from multiple sources.

"Wow that is impressive! You guys seem to be a few steps ahead of me! But would you tell me more about this CoP thing?" he asked, unsure of the meaning.

"As we may have stated before," Agent 13 began, *"CoP stands for Community of Practise, which is an effective way to create groups of passionate individuals who share an interest in PEOPLE, PROCESS, and PRODUCT. They foster collaboration and sharing of knowledge and are essential for a healthy DevOps mindset. It is a forum to be open-minded and candid, conducting discussions without fear of critique or punishment. The only idea or question that is bad in a CoP is the one that was never shared!"* He laughed. *"Agent 77 will delve into more details on CoPs later though."*

Agent 9 felt obligated to clarify Agent 13's quick overview.

"A main benefit of a CoP is that the participants help build relationships that promote sharing and learning from one another. More importantly, each member cultivates knowledge sharing, problem solving, re-use of experience and artefacts, and documentation of information that would otherwise be restricted to, what Agent 13 refers to as, a brain-on-a-stick." All the AoCs laughed, and Agent 13 gave him a thumbs up for the added details.

"Please encourage CoPs!" Agent 9 urged. *"It takes time and sustained effort, but you will reap the benefits of reduced duplication, cost and time, shared knowledge, trust and confidence in the long run."*

Barker was grateful for his decision to return to the Dock and seek the clarity he received. He was impressed by their knowledge and believed he grasped what the AoCs were talking about. He particularly liked the analogy of the boat taking a long and difficult journey. He understood that the passengers and crew may be new to the boat and journey, making it scary for all. He was confident in his "skipper's" ability to help select the right boat and steer the journey of discovery with DevOps through a path that would reduce the chances of capsizing.

"Thank you, Agents! Once again, you have provided very valuable information. May I state my key takeaways from our great discussion to ensure I captured it correctly?" he requested of the AoCs who attentively awaited his summary.

"So, in a nutshell," he began, itemizing on his fingers as he spoke.

*"We **start** with a **small** rowboat (such as a proof of concept or minimum viable product), and, as we cross a treacherous river successfully, we **move on** to a lake then oceans, **refining** and **building** a dedicated, committed, and cross-functional crew, aka team, which requires a **mindset** that **promotes** an atmosphere of **trust, accountability, responsibility, and transparency of issues**, so we can **accept challenges openly** and prepare for approaching storms, understanding that the boat may take on water or things may fall overboard, yet despite the mishaps, the crew will **reach the destination** and **celebrate as a team**."* He stopped to gauge the AoCs' reaction to his abridgment.

"Basically, without the team, we will sink and there may be no survivors," he finished, satisfied with his information recount.

The AoCs had nothing to add. It seemed that Barker had received the message, which elated them. They affirmed his thoughts, praised his interest and determination, and set a time for their next meeting.

Barker left the Dock, feeling much more grounded in the goal of the transformation. However, he felt that the other IT managers were either still not on board or unclear about the journey and that his new DevOps team and their mindset would require his management.

Returning to his office, he sent out several emails, describing how DevOps would be run in the IT Department and the mindset each member must have. In a meeting invite to the IT managers and other stakeholders, Barker also included several links to the DevOps internal Wiki for review. Then, he sketched out his collaboration plan on his whiteboard, which included his initial roadmap of a DevOps teams transformation plan, a detail considered long overdue by Maverick and the Overlords!

Team Commits to the Infamous 2AM Call

A Typical Disaster in the Making

Agent 13 received an urgent email from Knight, one of the operational leads, working on their DevOps program with Maverick, regarding a potential incident that DevOps might help remedy. After contacting Knight, he realised the seriousness of the incident and decided to go observe the live site room where operations was located.

Upon arrival, Agent 13 and Knight found the IT Operations (OPS) manager and Site Reliability Engineer (SRE), staring at an incident notification on a big screen labelled, 'Live Operational Events'. No one representing the business, leadership, IT development or security was present.

"This was a very serious incident," he thought. He said quietly to Knight, *"Why are these two frantically trying to go through the logs, look up the error codes and phone the suppliers alone?"* Knight winced and shook his head.

The first and most concerning issue Agent 13 noticed was their obvious struggle to understand the context of the incident. They flipped feverishly between email, dashboards and documentation from help desk support in search for clarity. Finding none, they eventually called the lead developer, who gave a hasty explanation of the probable issue, pointed them to a few logs, and ended the call without resolution, saying, *"We cannot reproduce the issue. We have never seen it before, and it works in our environment."*

Agent 13 wanted to help and spoke up to Knight again.

"Are you sure you have reviewed the right logs? Is this all of them? Why are the other stakeholders not here to help analyse the root cause and look for a remediation?" he asked in earnest.

Hearing these questions, the SRE and OPS manager gave him a disapproving look, prompting Agent 13 to return to observation mode. Knight was embarrassed; his colleagues were both rude and not transparent. Knight knew that he really was not welcome in this room either but could clearly help as part of the team that worked on the product.

The scene played out much like many others before it. After wasting hours, digging through documentation, it became evident that the logs were, indeed, not the right ones, and only the developers knew what the error codes meant.

Running out of options and pushing the incident from serious to critical, the OPS manager and SRE summoned the development team to join a call. Discussions and debates ensued, filled with hasty and futile assumptions. The call continued until they agreed on a probable cause and the recommendation that engineering create a 'quick fix'. Nevertheless, it was still unlikely to be quickly resolved due to operations' stringent processes, heavy governance and numerous approval flow, all in the name of quality and control.

None of this was new to Agent 13, who recognised that there was no chance for a 'quick fix' and speedy remediation without further frustrating business and, worse, the end-users. He had observed countless silos, wasted hours of context switching and escalations to arrange desperate, last minute changes in many IT departments.

These situations were exacerbated further by unnecessarily heavy governance, management approvals, interruptions, and blockers, producing desperation in the development team who felt hamstrung by operations.

The development team demanded more access to operational controls, live changes and direct intervention in a futile attempt to deploy their hotfix. In return, operations pushed back, concerned that their processes would not be followed, leaving the blame at their feet. The stalemate resulted in operations locking down privileged access even more and disengaging with other teams. This mindset cemented silos and replaced the last traces of collaboration with a toxic plume.

"Development and operations need to cooperate with each other," Agent 13 explained to Knight, *"They should share the same goals!"*

Once again, he witnessed two siloed teams, creating toxic environments rather than working together.

"We all must remove the toxicity before it kills any chance of collaboration!"

Reflecting on the 2AM Call

The next day, Maverick bumped into Agent 13 at breakfast. He had heard from Knight about the incident yesterday and tried to mediate and triage between the teams while waiting for the long, drawn out root cause analysis.

"Good morning, Agent 13," Maverick said in a cheerful manner. *"I heard about the incident yesterday you witnessed with Knight..."*

Agent 13 looked up from his tray with a serious expression.

"I did. May I be blunt? What I witnessed was, unfortunately, not uncommon. While observing your engineering teams, I realised several things, all regarding silos and walls in place.

1. *I noticed a wall between business and engineering.*
2. *There was no "we". Instead, support, engineering, operations, and business fostered unproductive "them and us" silos.*
3. *Additionally, there exists a large wall within the operations teams themselves."*

The two walked to a nearby table to sit down, continuing their conversation along the way.

"We need your and the rest of leadership's help, breaking down these silos by encouraging alignment of the teams toward your goals and supporting Lean organisational governance," Agent 13 stated. *"Otherwise, your teams will drown in a turbulent and toxic sea!"*

There was silence while Agent 13 and Maverick ate their breakfast, both consumed in thought. After a final swig of coffee, Maverick said, *"You have my full support, but please elaborate on what you and the other AoCs suggest."*

"Remember when we discussed the lines of alignment and autonomy?" Agent 13 asked. *"Well, the reason we introduced this early in our meetings is because everyone in the organisation must understand and respect the lines of alignment and autonomy."* He wiped his face and placed his napkin on his tray.

"This is critical for the DevOps mindset. Departments, teams and the entire organisation will enjoy their autonomy, working collectively in their own way. This mindset brings everyone together and promotes cultural alignment, which leads to harmony and improves the chances of success for the organisation's shared vision and goals. Governance should be Lean.

"When we work as one team and shed the silos, we avoid shuffling responsibility, blaming others, and creating an air of toxicity!" he

informed, glad to have been given the opportunity to discuss his observations first thing.

Maverick felt partially responsible for this issue. He had always encouraged healthy competition, which was, unintentionally, fostering silos in his own IT departments.

"Since first introducing DevOps here, I have observed the development teams embrace some Lean principles, starting the journey of continuous delivery," he praised. *"The development team has created and used key performance indicators, such as Lead Time for Change and Deployment Frequency, resulting in many improvements. Operations has made great strides with their key performance indicators as well, such as with Mean Time to Recovery and Change Failure Rate,"* he added, increasing the smile on Maverick's face.

However," he cautioned. Maverick's smile faded in anticipation of what would follow. *"All of this will continue to be impeded by OPS, viewing releases as large deployments rather than small releases of value,"* he warned an anxious Maverick, who remained silent, waiting for further elaboration. *"So, instead of creating nimble releases, they will continue to produce less nimble super-tankers."*

"Part of the rationale for OPS' view of large releases is based on manual and intangible processes, checklists, and approvals," defended Maverick, embarrassed by Agent 13's report.

"Understood, but that is something we need to move away from in order to unlock performance, quality, safety and sustainability," coached Agent 13.

"Yes, yes. I remember those points and links to DevOps in the DORA Research paper I reviewed some time ago," Maverick recalled.

Figure 19 - The infamous 2AM Call

"Correct," Agent 13 sustained. *"Which brings me to the core of the DevOps mindset; the 2AM call. This is an issue with the product that arises suddenly, and typically, at an inconvenient time, hence its moniker. If handled properly, using a DevOps mindset, it follows the principle that enables your organisation to delight the customer and unlock collaboration. It is pivotal to bringing everyone together in a customer-focused, value-first, product supported by a vibrant DevOps mindset!"* he described.

Maverick was interested in the points Agent 13 was highlighting.

Agent 13 interpreted his interest as a green light to continue, asking, *"During the next live site incident, may we, the AoCs, encourage and nurture a culture of team accountability?"*

"Of course, you can! In fact, we would welcome it!" Maverick exclaimed, seizing the opportunity for expert assistance.

"Great!" Agent 13 said, thrilled with Maverick's willingness. *"It is so important for everyone to feel responsible, accountable, and committed to solve the problem. This spirit of cooperation focuses everyone on analysing the root cause and working together to mitigate the issue quickly as one team."*

Maverick made a few more notes then continued to stare at his paper. *"I'm not so sure I feel comfortable with everyone being involved in root cause analysis,"* he admitted to himself.

"Especially, since many individuals in operations and support are contracted resources."

Maverick looked up at Agent 13 and tried to deflect the whole team concept. *"We have the Site Reliability Engineers. Can they not own and drive the live site incidents to resolution? Then share the results with the teams?"* he offered instead.

Agent 13 did not respond immediately. He recalled a conversation with Agent 77 during the 2AM call discussion where they had both agreed that sharing lessons learned was equally as important as it was to discover the reason for and solution to the incident. This could not occur without a 'whole team' mindset. It required the unified team to action change and avoid the problem in the first place. If so, it could result in:

- Improved and effective testing – fail early.
- Boosted quality during early product lifecycle – shift left.
- Reduced technical debt – focus on features.
- Saved costs – reinvest in engineering system.

Thus, the value of the 2AM call extended beyond those who found the problem and fixed it.

"We have found measurable and proven value when representatives or members from development, security, QA, business, and operations are actively involved in future 2AM calls. Further, we have determined that everyone, including leadership, must be in the call chain to promote transparency and avoid the need for escalations.

"For example, everyone has 5 minutes to join during office hours, and 15 minutes after hours. It is imperative that everyone remains engaged until the root cause is revealed and mitigated, knowing it is not over until we receive a smile and confirmation from a delighted end-user!" Agent 13 sat back in his chair, waiting for Maverick's reaction.

Maverick considered the perspective. *"So, the 2AM call is really about the team coming together at the time to fix the problem then again later to look for ways to avoid it from recurring?"* Agent 13 nodded and Maverick contemplated a bit more before continuing, *"When I think of the 2AM call, I picture a developer – exhausted, inconvenienced, and annoyed – getting a call from the help desk at 2AM. I would think that, alone, would motivate them to, not only, fix the problem but proactively try to avoid it happening in the first place!"*

Agent 13 laughed, *"Exactly! Remember, it is a collaborative team effort. You will be amazed by how the overall quality bar is raised once the whole team has endured a few 2AM calls!"*

Effective organisations have collaborative teams who embrace the 2AM call as an opportunity to learn and improve! Timely and thorough root-cause analysis, remediation and transparent communication are key. Assigning blame and unsubstantiated, shallow answers are anti-patterns that must be weeded out!

In Lean practise, there is a notion of the Andon cord, which means that when a quality problem is detected on the assembly line, the Andon cord is pulled, stopping the entire assembly line, requiring everyone to gather to fix the problem before the line resumes. This is a hard lesson, resulting in lowered cost and improved quality!

"The 2AM call does not end with a resolution. Rather, it carries forward a sharing of the outcomes. A good place to do so while also introducing the notion of a culture of learning and innovation is through a community of practise where learnings from recent incidents are discussed and techniques and advice on how to avoid them are shared. CoPs provide an opportunity to build and nurture relationships, which, in turn, promotes the idea that everyone needs be a Service Reliability Engineer, at heart." Agent 13 advised.

Maverick was in full agreement with Agent 13. His concerns about the "whole team" concept were replaced by his newfound understanding of the benefits.

"Great chat. It makes sense to be transparent and engage with our users, so they will be far more understanding, tolerant, and patient with the process," Maverick admitted.

The two tidied up the table and headed back to their respective workspaces to begin the workday.

DevOps Mindset Value 2 Goal Reached

 Well done, reader! We have reached our second goal: **Value stakeholders and their feedback** rather than simply adapting to change.

You cannot buy and install DevOps, nor can you buy and install transformation for any business. Making change happen, especially with a DevOps mindset means we need to learn, engage, accept and value our stakeholders; their concerns and their needs. Even when we do not agree or have different priorities, fixing a perceived or real problem by one person or team without discussing the solution with our colleagues, outside of our team, group, our department can be costly and have negative consequences. There is never time for politics when delighting our customers!

Obviously, one should strive to reduce, even eradicate, the infamous 2AM calls with the idea that this is only a triage to serious problems. Most importantly, however, we must realise that there will always be bugs, issues, and live site incidents. Rather than treating the situation as an exercise to light our hair on fire, use it as an exercise in embracing the problem or situation as an opportunity to learn and improve with all our stakeholders starting with Development and Operations.

Barker showed us that there is no room for micro-management or the "my-way-or-the-highway" mentality. Instead, we should inspire and empower everyone we work with. Try to use inspirational communication and accept failures as opportunities to learn and improve, using collaboration, responsibility, pride, and accountability.

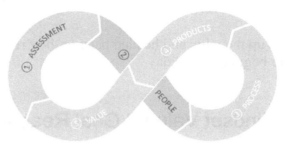

See 5 essential values for the DevOps mindset (Agent 13 & 77, 2019) and Community of Practise14, and the Creating a successful Community of Practise (CoP) event (AoC, 2020) checklist.4

The Dock

Agent 13 met up with the team at the Dock and relayed his conversation with Maverick. The AoCs all acknowledged that the teams working with Maverick and Barker were starting to buy into the mindset, showing inklings of adoption. There was consensus that the teams were beginning to realise the importance of PEOPLE.

Agent 13 began, *"We have ticked off the second goal of the DevOps mindset. The lack of collaboration is a big challenge for Maverick and Barker to solve.*

*"We must coach them both to be supportive and inspirational, while also enforcing the organisation's governance. We also need to join all future 2AM calls and ensure they analyse the root cause and mitigate the issue **as a team**."*

Agent 77 added, *"Yes, let us suggest this to the leadership to garner their support. Getting trust in place for people to experiment, learn and share their feelings and thoughts creates a safe environment to allow people to become awesome!*

"I also agree that we should listen in on the conversations and provide guidance on good governance as processes are being adapted to the Agile and DevOps ways of working. The 2AM call and your findings at OPS is likely just a hint of some of the rapids, rocks and sharks, awaiting this boat we call DevOps transformation."

Agent 9 sat quietly, reflecting before chiming in, *"The 2AM call is at the core of the DevOps mindset. Sometimes the journey (DevOps) can be painful (2AM calls). However, a little pain can be a great teacher!"*

Boat Inspection

Toxicity - Where Politics Trump Culture

On his way home for the evening, Agent 13 decided to stop by Barker's office to say goodbye.

Barker was just outside his office, in a common work area, finishing up a discussion with the development team about a project. There were raised voices and objections, and the new Scrum Master that belonged to another project was present. This particular project was not the "Pilot" one chosen for the DevOps transformation.

Agent 13 stood unnoticed in Barker's office doorway, listening intently. He could hear and see another toxic atmosphere forming.

After the discussion, Barker noticed him and invited him to sit down privately in his office.

Agent13 frowned. *"Tell me, Barker, does this team own the HOW and WHEN of your project?"* he asked, redundantly.

Barker looked nervous. He knew this conversation was headed right back to the line of alignment and autonomy.

Agent 13 continued, *"When your team was discussing scheduling and project timelines, I noticed you wrote fixed delivery dates on the white board and referenced a fixed schedule on your roadmap presentation. Who defined those?"*

Barker hesitated then answered, *"I am given dates by the business, which I cannot change. I made sure that everyone seemed to understand WHAT the project was and WHY it was important, which is on your line of alignment and autonomy magnet."* Barker proudly pointed to the Line of Alignment and Autonomy whiteboard magnet the AoCs had given him.

"I also took to heart your point on information radiators so that anyone interested in this project can view a clearly articulated vision posted in our common coffee area, next to a list of delivery milestones..." he informed. *"And, to top it off, I made sure that both Automaton and Boundless share their DevOps learning as active members of the development and test teams, which will form a community of practise in the near future to passionately share knowledge and contribute to technical manifestos, I hope,"* Barker triumphantly rambled.

Barker was pleased with himself, feeling that he had fulfilled the DevOps mindset. He had taken on the role of a semi-quasi Product Owner to encourage the team to collaborate better. However, unintentionally, he only partially filled that role due to his sole concern being on the IT pieces of work needing completion. Using words, like *"there's a concern"* and *"that's a real problem"* without sharing details or making suggestions on how to address them,

Barker attempted to demonstrate that he was in control of his team and his project.

He did not realise that his mannerisms and attitude made his points neither actionable nor encouraging for the team. The dynamic reeked of toxic waste and mistrust, putting off many of the engineers, whether they reported to him or not.

Barker stated his appreciation for the team while also asking them to work extra hours to meet strategic milestones and implement key technologies. He became side-tracked by new technology, overwhelmed by the conflict of a fixed budget and deadline expectations from the leadership. Out of habit, he moved back to the "command and control" position and resumed dictating what, when, how and why.

This made the team overwhelmed, leaving them with a lack of understanding and sense of dread. They were forced to do the work when Barker wanted it, not when it was feasible. Even with the Scrum Master present, Barker and the team were not breaking down their product into a backlog and collectively agreeing to a healthy and sustainable delivery cadence.

This resulted in a pseudo Agile way of working where everyone pretended to embrace agility while being forced to chase traditional deadlines. The team never showed any appetite to consider feedback, respond to change, demonstrate transparency, or extend trust.

Agent 13 was aware of Barker's attempts as well as his shortcomings. He explained these to Barker, who initially went red in the face and became defensive. However, Agent 13 continued to use proactive language, demonstrate empathy, and use win:win coaching by:

- Asking questions
- Talking straight
- Showing respect
- Focusing on win:win conversations

This diffused Barker's defensiveness and allowed him to reflect. In fact, having this critical conversation ended up being helpful to Barker. He remained thankful for the AoCs' interest in his projects, even if they seemed out of scope from their deliverables and contract.

Agent 13 addressed the fact that the culture of fear had taken hold of most, if not all, of the team. Stakeholders, such as leadership, had influenced team members on the HOW and WHEN, taking away a sense of empowerment and trust.

As Agent 13 described a concerning picture of everyone working extra hours or desperately trying to get off the project, which had created a toxic cloud of team fear and inevitable project failure, Barker walked over and grabbed his Line of Alignment and Autonomy magnet and began fiddling with it in his hand.

He was aware that he had been meddling below the line of autonomy and authority yet continued his "command and control" style as a delivery micro-manager instead of a supportive leader and product owner. He recognised that he also represented the end-user, who had lost a voice in the project. Then, Barker suddenly realised that he was likely losing trust with the team, including the project manager!

At this, Barker stopped fidgeting with the magnet and looked at Agent 13 with pleading eyes.

He let out a laugh, *"Go ahead, Agent 13. Say it!"*

Agent 13 shrugged and said, *"You need to respect the line of autonomy! You only own the WHAT and WHY! Your team owns the HOW and WHEN! You must, for the sake of everyone, trust the team!"*

Barker nodded repeatedly. *"How should we engage product owners, the Scrum Master (team lead) and other roles?"* he inquired.

Emphasising that this was a larger discussion, Agent 13 said, *"The organisation, departments and team must work with the product* owner, Scrum Master (team lead), and rest of the stakeholders to understand the concept of autonomy, self-organisation, and self-management. These concepts are core to the Agile practise and DevOps mindset. Leaders must encourage and ensure that everyone respects the line of ownership.

"Otherwise, the toxicity in the environment will worsen and possibly kill any chance of improving their current state. A toxic environment can be subtle almost like carbon-monoxide, that is, invisible but deadly. This creates culture of blaming, stifling innovation. People will hear and follow the common theme of "that is the way we do things here" and thus change, innovation, improvement is ignored.

"If the toxic cloud continues to grow and move across teams, they will feel unempowered, uninspired, and untrusted. Infected teams will be unable to hold themselves accountable and responsible for their features. Worse still, the team's passion will likely degrade to resigned silence, with everyone putting in extra time in the false hope of meeting the enforced milestones. This causes poor health, leading people to avoid the team and the work, which may eventually result in them leaving the organisation altogether."

Barker concurred, putting the magnet back on the whiteboard. *"What do you do about people who refuse or resist change?"* he asked in seriousness.

"Folks like Umpty?" Agent 13 guessed.

Barker nodded, thinking about how at his wits end he was with some of the folks who were not motivated to change or were subtlety resisting.

"When you find yourself in one of these toxic projects with an Umpty and there is no appetite for change, you usually have only one choice. Jump overboard!" Agent 13 stated.

"To quote Agent 77: 'You cannot force change, only coach, lead and support it.' There are many coaching tactics to help identify the rationale and reasons why people resist change, but that is also a much larger discussion. We can help with that, though, if you would

like. You need to be healthy, both at work and away from it, and I can see this is adding unnecessary stress and burden that should not be taken on alone," observed Agent 13.

"But I am the manager! This is my job, and Umpty is my staff!" Barker challenged.

"I know that, but it does not mean you are alone. We are here to guide you, not take away responsibility from you. As a friend and coach, I suggest that you make sure you prioritise family time and personal wellness," Agent 13 recommended. *"And, if things get too difficult, assign another manager or project to that person, when possible, as a last resort."*

Their conversation was interrupted by one of Barker's staff members, knocking on his door. The two quickly wrapped up with promises of revisiting the discussion soon.

Act 3

PROCESS - Small Agile Strokes

And Another Morning Chat

After a few turbulent days with teams in silos and Dev vs. Ops, Agents 77 and 13 decided to bring a platter of coffee and donuts to Big Corp to boost morale. As usual, they had a vibrant discussion along the way.

Agent 13 was thinking about the DevOps pipeline, complexities, and the dynamics of all the interactions and connections. There was potential for waste from project concept to delivery during a typical project.

"Assuming a gated, Waterfall release process exists, consisting of the Opportunity Analysis, Product Planning, Product Construction, Transition to GA, Deploy and Monitor phases, how would you move to a more iterative release process, releasing code every 2 weeks?" consulted Agent 13.

This was a deep and complex subject that required some thought before responding. Agent 77, thinking intently, tripped but managed not to spill the precious tray of coffees.

"A fully developed DevOps mindset takes time," he stated, readjusting the coffees in the tray. *"Just like a great product or idea; improvements happen incrementally. There is no single big bang to your solution. Incidentally, Agent 9 and I were discussing a method to move to a more iterative release process called Vertical Slicing.*

"Vertical Slicing *is the art of cutting scope into more meaningful chunks (slices) that add business value when consumable and stood independently and incrementally. A vertical slice helps release value into the hands of the customer, quickly.*

"Thus, the phases you described above – Opportunity Analysis, Product Planning, Construction, Transition and Release to the customer *– all require good application of the DevOps mindset, which means regular feedback and **no silos**. In situations where we have some reasonable assumptions or known value of the product, feature or enhancement, we may want to introduce MBIs (Minimum Business Increment Al Shaloway, Flex 2019).*

"To quote Agent 9: 'The thinner you slice your stories, the more:

- *Potential for clarity there is around the scope of work*
- *Precise estimates tend to be. A thinner slice means a faster feedback loop.*
- *Iterative your release process becomes*
- *Business value is generated sooner*
- *Efficient release-wise your teams become'*

"The art of vertical slicing is easier said than done but, once mastered, can be the enabler to increasing release cadence," Agent 77 finished as they approached the building.

"The bigger question here is: should the goal be to release consumables software every 2 weeks? Would you feel safe on a plane or boat that you knew had to release software every 2 weeks, no matter what? The genesis of releasing code every 2 weeks is to help minimize delivery risks by shortening the cycle and releasing frequently. However, for critical life or regulatory issues, you may want to review which software is released and how often. Thus, if releasing code frequently increases a safety risk, would you still want to do it?" Agent 13 proposed.

They walked past a newsstand, noting the irony within the latest headline: "*New software glitch found in Boeing's troubled 737 Max jet*" (David Koenig, Associated Press, 2019).

The First DevOps Meeting with IT Managers

Barker took to heart that he needed to get more involved with his stakeholders. Therefore, Barker hosted the first round of the DevOps Program talks with his business leaders and IT managers. He had not invited the Agents of Chaos, but when Maverick found out; he insisted they be present to observe as flies on the wall.

The business was not overly happy with IT due to its perceived slow support. Divisions were starting to form across IT as well due to some managers, treating the DevOps Program as the latest fad and pretending it was not real.

At the meeting, the AoCs and Barker sensed tension crackling in the air. The AoCs had quietly entered on the side of the room, observing the people and proceedings with a pinch of awe and anxiety for Barker, Maverick and the program.

"Do you think Barker and Maverick have taken our mentorship, guidance, and critical feedback to heart?" Agent 13 asked the other AoCs in a whisper. *"Do you think they will emphasise the importance of people over process and products, or will more silos form and divisions widen?"*

The others looked at him and shrugged. *"Let's wait and see!"* they replied with their fingers crossed.

Barker stood in front of a large screen behind a podium. He cleared his throat with a nervous cough and opened the meeting.

"I want to thank you all for coming. By now, you should be well aware that IT has started a DevOps Program. Maverick and I need your help and support to make this a success. We appreciate you all working together with our DevOps team. Some of you have asked who is leading the effort, and I am pleased to announce that I am assigning Redline to kick off the first DevOps project to start our digital transformation. I am sure all of you are tired of hearing and talking about Agile and DevOps transformations. So, let's start by more doing and less talking."

One of the IT leaders raised his hand and asked, *"I have heard this referred to as a pilot and a project. Which is it?"*

A sudden hush fell across the room. The AoCs looked at the leader who asked the question, thinking that he was clearly unhappy not to have been selected to lead this DevOps initiative.

Agent 13 whispered, *"I wonder how Barker is going to handle this."*

Barker did not like this particular person in the IT department, nor did he care for the diminishing connotation of his question. *"It's both!"* he snapped. *"It's a Pilot Project!"* He then looked at the AoCs, who nodded apprehensively.

The whole room was silent and uncomfortable. The AoCs made notes for a discussion with Barker afterwards.

- Emotive responses and terms like "less talking and more doing" sound exciting but can create friction and divide or alienate folks in the room.
- The focus on the project is misplaced as projects are part of the journey, not the journey itself.

Another IT leader who had been around longer at Big Corp then Barker, broke the silence in the room by saying, *"Look, we understand that this DevOps Pilot Project is very important to you. However, we are just too busy right now with key delivery milestones in progress for two major releases. I do not feel comfortable committing resources to this DevOps Pilot right now. Perhaps, we can revisit after the releases next month or even later, preferably?"*

Barker's heart sunk, and the AoCs saw several sharks, lurking in the room. They had expected a challenge getting everyone onboard, but they did not expect colleagues to try to stop the DevOps program altogether.

"Yeah, and I need some of Redline's time! She is my most efficient developer," another leader called out. *"Only she understands the application architecture. I need her to help us with these releases!"*

The AoCs looked at each other while Agent 9 noted additional items for discussion:

- *Lack of transparency*
- *Divisions and Silos*
- *Deadlines*
- *Waterfall mindset*
- *No mention of people and culture*

Barker sensed a coup about to start and worried his meeting would go off the rails. "*Alright, alright,*" he conceded, putting his hands up in mock-surrender. *"Our DevOps Pilot will not require dedicated or full-time resources, it's optional. Okay?"*

The managers all seemed to take a collective deep breath, smiling at each other with wide shark grins. They were not taking the DevOps transformation seriously, still viewing it as another flavour of the month. They picked over the goodies and coffee before leaving the room. Barker, embarrassed by the lack of buy-in from his teams, avoided the AoCs' stares, slumped his head and left the room slowly.

"*Here we go. It seems we are starting the transformation on a slippery slope with lots of rocks and sharks in our path to adoption. Not the best discussion and decisions made today,*" remarked Agent 77.

 "*Nope, not at all,*" sighed Agent 9 in agreement.

Agent 13 shook his head, "*This approach is definitely not ideal. However, with an opportunity to sow the right seeds and bring the stakeholders together, we can, as always, make it work.*"

A few managers stayed behind chatting, and the AoCs overheard one ask, "*Aren't we already doing DevOps?*"

As the AoCs left to head back to the Dock, they heard a collective chime from an email Barker had just sent out. It was marked urgent, stating that an IT leader had just employed a Scrum Master in another IT department, planning to implement Agile Scrum based deliveries.

The AoCs were not alarmed, happy to include any fellow Agilist in their DevOps adoption plans. However, to some, DevOps seemed to conflict with other Agile approaches, so they thought it best to meet and consult with the Scrum Master. They all agreed that with the Scrum Master's help and insight, they would be able to explore that department's agility and possibly gain another advocate for Agile change.

"I am not sure how you guys feel, but I have the sensation of turbulent waters ahead. I also saw a dorsal shark fin circling our puny rowboat and no sign of the coast guard," Agent 13 confessed to the others as they walked back to the Dock.

The AoCs chuckled at his analogy but agreed that there were, indeed, sharks in the vicinity and rapids up ahead. Developing a DevOps mindset was not going to be easy, although it rarely was!

Just then, Agent 13 received a text message from Barker, stating, *"Maverick is on his way. He wants an update on the 2AM discussion we had, and I think he also wants to chat about today's IT Management meeting."*

"You know, now that I think about it, I did not see Maverick at the meeting this morning, which is interesting," Agent 9 remarked.

Agent 9's observation lingered in the air, weighing heavy on their minds. They decided to have a quick huddle before Maverick joined them.

"With the conversation around roles, dedicated vs non dedicated team members, and this new Scrum Master joining another IT department, I have been thinking even more about Agile and DevOps

ways of working and roles. Agent 77, what do you think, can Scrum Master, Team Lead, and manager roles be shared?" Agent 9 queried.

Agent 77 considered the question.

"Some roles can be shared, such as the Team Lead or Scrum Master also being a team member or the Architect Owner. However, I would not recommend a person new to Agile as a Team Lead. A Team Lead should be a well-seasoned Scrum Master who can guide and coach the team. They support the Product Owner by being available anytime to ensure all roadblocks are being taken care of under the leadership of the Product Owner," replied Agent 77.

"That makes sense and is why we educate on the roles, rights and responsibilities to the team and their stakeholders," Agent 9 concurred.

"That's right. It is also why we put this information on a Wiki for reference as a baseline for this information," Agent 77 added. *"While we do not suggest a Product Owner share the same role as the Team Lead, a senior developer or engineer with Agile experience and education can make an excellent one.*

"However, it is important to note that Team Leads are not managers. But if a manager wants to become a Team Lead, that is fine too, as long as they support the Product Owner of the What, and the team of the How," reminded Agent 77.

Agent 9 drew a line from Project Manager to Product Owner. *"Let's finish up this diagram and get it up on the Wiki, so we can educate Barker and the team sooner than later,"* he proposed.

Reflecting on 2AM Call and Dedication

Maverick stopped in as anticipated, and the AoCs showed him the Dock covered with information radiators. They had a Kanban board on the left wall and a large, 65-inch touch screen with scrolling dashboards on the right wall, which was used to present and as electronic whiteboard.

Maverick also noticed large post-it notes stuck to the back wall with a number of drawings (models) that the AoCs used in the Wiki, its URL written on the wall and in the corner of the large screen. He made a note of it on his phone, remembering the AoCs had sent this along with his personal dashboard and Wiki page.

The AoCs had spent time, designing their work area to make everyone feel welcomed and informed about what was going on. They had requested a small budget and space to design a common work area at the beginning of the project.

The room was made special by its location and the precious visualisation of the good, the bad, and the ugly. The AoCs made sure it was situated centrally to the business, architecture, security, operations, and development hideouts. Everyone knew where it was, walking past it several times per day, which reinforced that transparency since access to information and communication was key.

"Good morning, everyone! I wanted to drop by for an update on the Retrospective of the recent 2AM incident call? What happened? Which team failed in such a disastrous way? Given the Overlords have approved this DevOps project, I'm not sure what to report. This is really bad!"

The AoCs were slightly stunned by Maverick asking them about an incident unrelated to their project and the fact that, despite the lack of collective buy-in, the small fledgling DevOps team was progressing nicely.

"Did Agent 13 not fill you in at breakfast?" asked Agent 77.

Maverick's face changed from cheerful to angry.

"I expect you AoCs to get everyone on board and find out where the problems are! Clearly, the DevOps project that I am funding is not working!" he shouted. When the AoCs did not reply, Maverick composed himself, realising that he was aiming his frustrations at the wrong team. Nonetheless, he wanted to find out who *was* responsible for the problem, and who was going to fix it, now!

Calmly, Agent 13 stated, *"Maverick, I am due for another coffee. Shall we walk and talk to update you on the progress we are making with the DevOps team and the 2AM conversation we had?"*

Maverick agreed, humbly offering, *"My apologies, Agents. You can see I am frustrated. Let's walk and talk, Agent 13."*

"No offense, but part of a DevOps mindset is collaboration, transparency and respect. Thus, an anti-pattern to this mindset would be to walk in the room, as you did, and fire accusatory questions," Agent 13 chided. *"DevOps is teams coming together, working on common goals and supporting each other in a culture of learning, innovation and improvement. This is why we must bring safety into the equation to make everyone feel comfortable to experiment and fail fast. We can only do that if you and the other leaders promote a blameless culture."*

Maverick hated to admit that he had been wrong but knew that was the case. After considering how to acknowledge this fact, he said, *"Your point is taken, and yes there is an issue of blaming others in our organisation. The Overlords blame me and the whole IT department for many things, which causes us to behave, well, less than stellar. You are right, Agent 13. The DevOps and Agile books correlate with your guidance, charging leaders with communicating in an inspirational way and stimulating teams intellectually, which will only come by nurturing a supportive leadership."*

"I am glad you feel this way, Maverick, because when you first said, 'this is really bad,' it shocked and reminded me of one of my old managers, who often used the same demotivating comment. He was neither a leader, nor an inspiration. In fact, I ended up taking a two-month sabbatical because I was so demotivated and burnt out with

the fear of failure. I had developed a hatred for the career I had loved for more than thirty years," Agent 13 confessed, soulfully.

The two remained quiet while finishing up their coffee preparations. As they headed back to the Dock, the conversation resumed.

"Do you remember what Agent 77 said about culture?" Agent 13 quizzed. *"He said, 'Leaders are responsible for the culture of their organisation they represent. It is through leadership who, by example, demonstrates the culture and behaviour of the organisations they work for, encouraging their teams, staff and stakeholders as a champion',"* he recalled before Maverick could reply.

"It takes courage to speak out like you did just now," acknowledged Maverick. *"I respect you for doing so, and in private, I might add. I really appreciate you and the AoCs for being open and straight with me. We have been so indoctrinated with failure not being an option that we obviously have a lot to change."*

As the two arrived at the Dock, Maverick saw Barker and his team, collaborating with the other AoCs, in deep discussion. He watched the dashboard and recognised the Goals, Questions, Metrics (GQM) the AoCs had originally setup and used in the survey some months ago. He realised the data was up to date, but they were not hitting some key objectives. Maverick excused himself, heading back to his office to review the unaddressed or outdated findings with the Overlords. He knew that the organizational GQMs and IT priorities needed to be reviewed to ensure the dashboard was up to date and could be measured with. He planned to update the dashboard with the AoCs' help and roll out another poll or survey to gather feedback with his IT management team, which included Barker.

Agent 13 joined the AoCs who were deep into their story development and backlog. He had missed the Retrospective, however he scanned all the key points raised on one of the walls while Agent 77 updated the dashboard – Retrospective area, which contained some content that was private for just team members and other key points ready to be shared to various stakeholders through Barker and the Wiki.

Agent 13 noticed key points from the 2AM call had been captured as well as the challenge of dedicated teams. He was happy that feedback and documenting was working. He watched as Barker reviewed the next sprint with the team.

Barker realised that he needed dedicated, self-organising members to become a more effective team. It was a huge mindset shift for him that triggered several questions.

- What are the next steps?
- What about the other managers who are using his resources?
- Are they still his resources?
- Who do the team members follow in a self-organising team?
- Are there implications for human resources and unions?

Checkout the Positive and negative characteristics of self-organising teams (AoC, 2020) checklist , and the Create a self-formed team with Post-Its (AoC, 2020) walk-through, to get you started.

Barker posed the questions to the AoCs and his core DevOps team. The dedicated resource issue was the biggest challenge.

"*I need some help,*" Redline said as she turned to look at Knight. "*It is difficult to get the whole team together. We are all so busy with other projects, and some of us only report to Barker in a dotted line.*"

"I know," nodded Knight. *"Perhaps, we can ask one of the coaches to help us get approval from Barker and our managers to focus solely on the stories for this sprint or iteration or whatever it is called. I can never remember which to use,"* Knight admitted.

"Either is okay," she informed. *"Looking at the backlog and priorities, this seems like it would go much faster if we were dedicated, otherwise we may not be able to finish what we commit to."*

Barker looked at the stories and tasks required to complete a piece of work that would become releasable and consumable. He had not yet received estimates from the team, but he knew this was a tall order to complete, especially since he already had been given deadlines by Maverick and the business.

Redline continued, *"Although the AoCs put the roles, goals and phases up on our Wiki and created a backlog with Barker, we had not agreed on the roles for the team and yet we are already moving to another iteration in the inception phase."*

Barker winced, but the AoCs were pleased to see this discussion organically going in the right direction, with no need for them to chime in. Good coaches watch how things play out and guide only when necessary, at the right time.

Knight asked, *"Have we agreed on who will be the Product Owner?"* looking from Redline to Barker.

"Barker, it's you because you're the manager of this project, right?"

Barker nodded yes, but the AoCs flashed up roles on the dashboard, so everyone could clearly see that the Product Owner was not necessarily the default role for the manager. Agent 9's drawing of the roles included a clear line from traditional roles, such as Project Manager, Business Application Owner and others, pointing to the role. In this case, the Business Owner and Project Manager for this piece of work was Barker, who was very much up for the job.

Barker surveyed the responsibilities of the Product Owner more carefully, glancing over this initially in the "Choose Your WoW Book." This time, he realised they were much more cumbersome than he imagined. His eyes widened with awareness.

"Barker, you are always so busy. Based on the roles in Wiki, I think the PO role is a full-time job! I am happy to help you with it!" Knight offered with a large smile.

Barker looked at the team and said, *"I **am** very busy. However, I need to work with the AoCs and Maverick to examine how we can become more dedicated to this iteration and beyond."* He knew that this was going to be a long road and that they were not all going to be dedicated team members.

Rabbit, who was not officially part of the team, asked to join the meeting, convinced she needed to be dedicated to the team. She quickly wrote an email, asking her manager for permission to get involved as a dedicated member. Although hesitant to lose a resource for the next two weeks, her manager allowed it, clearly not wanting to be left out of the trendy new DevOps transformation, which would leave all the credit to Barker.

Barker began to write down the team members' names, assigning official roles in the project.

- Barker – Product Owner
- Redline – Team Lead and Senior Developer
- Knight – Architect Owner, Solution Architect / Operations
- Team Members - TBD

He then spoke to the team individually, regarding what team member(s) to recruit for the next piece of work. At the same time, Rabbit grabbed Agent 9's attention off to the side,

"*Agent 9, Agent 9!*" Rabbit nervously called out.

"Yes? What can I do for you?"

Rabbit frowned, saying, "*My team is working on new features for a different software product in another line of business. There are several requirements that sound similar and overlap work that Barker has on his backlog.*"

"*Hmm,*" Agent 9 said, *"We discussed sharing across teams and departments with Barker and Maverick. This sounds like a good time to create the concept of a Community Meetup, to lay the foundation for a community of practise!"*

"Wow, that sounds really cool! Where can I find out more about this?" asked Rabbit, energised by the news.

"The concept of the Community of Practise is in the Choose your WoW book, and we have added it to the Wiki as well. Each implementation is specific to the team and organisation where it is setup because it is voluntary. I will discuss it with my fellow AoCs and the other teams and get back to you with a draft manifesto, like terms of reference to help put scope, objectives and other key starting points for this to launch successfully."

"That sounds great! I would love to be involved and share our experiences and ideas! Thank you," Rabbit exclaimed before bouncing off quickly as she normally did.

Agent 9 inserted some additional thoughts to the CoP section of their DevOps Pilot Wiki, adding:

```
As leaders and agents of change, we need to
enable and encourage people to collaborate,
```

explore, innovate, and unlock their motivation in a safe and supportive environment. Nurture activities such as crisp daily stand-ups, demonstrations, inspect & adapt workshops, software engineering dojos, lunch & learns, and off-site team building to recognise everyone's commitment, highlight success stories, and foster communication. This fuels awareness and learning, identifies potential duplication and re-use of work, and creates a sense of unity.

He included references to the definition found in Wikipedia, the Choose your WoW book and others. Then, he and Agent 77 discussed the goal of Improve your WoW (Disciplined Agile, 2019) and Grow Your Team Members (Disciplined Agile, 2020), which provides decisions and options for both the CoP and sharing, evolving and growing your teams.

Time to Launch the Community

During his next meeting with his fellow Agents, Agent 9 discussed scheduling the first community workshop.

"Agents, given my conversation with Rabbit and the potential for both projects sharing, I think it is time to launch a CoP, starting with a Meetup. To begin, here is a list of things to consider as we help create a Community Meetup:

- *Ensure we have a clear purpose and modus operandi. Refine and reinforce it continuously.*
- *Ensure we deliver value to the members and organisation.*
- *Blend into the organisation's culture and keep it simple!*
- *Nurture leaders, not followers.*
- *Discourage virtual participation – face to face is most effective.*
- *Emphasise that this is a volunteer-based, not mandated community."*

"Looks good, Agent 9," the others commended. *"I also suggest that we let everyone know this is a safe place to learn and experiment. While we may discover good ways of working (patterns) and anti-patterns, all options, subjects, and viewpoints are valid. Everyone has a say and is equal in sharing and collaboration. This is also a good time for managers to become leaders by enabling, supporting and observing,"* Agent 77 pointed out.

Agent 9 added those to the draft Wiki CoP under Meetup guidelines, which will form a term of reference or manifesto.

"Great additions, Agent 77. Everyone needs to view the CoP as an opportunity to learn and share, exploring and trying DevOps practises that will help us become more data driven through embracing validated learning and improve the key performance indicators that are agreed upon by the leadership and teams."

"Exactly. In fact, the Retrospectives and our Guided Continuous Innovation and Improvement will link directly to effective CoPs for sharing what is working and what is not. The CoP also can help improve measuring and collating data across groups, departments and the organisation," Agent 77 informed.

Agent 13 added, *"In the future, we may suggest Big Corp consider creating more focused CoPs, such as Agile Ways of Working in Product Management, Engineering, and Operations."*

"DevOps is a mindset that takes effort, and there will be many opportunities to inspect, adapt, and share transparently. We need to continuously streamline our DevOps practises and embrace failure as an opportunity to learn and innovate," Agent 9 reminded no one in particular.

The AoCs continued to discuss how to seed today's discussion topics to add potential value to all the represented teams. They agreed to highlight the need for and challenge of built-in quality. They decided to focus on topics that would open up silos, demonstrate value to everyone in the audience and enable both development and operations to lay the foundations for continuous integration, delivery, testing, configuration and infrastructure as code, and unified pipelines.

They also realised that, while it would be great to invite all the stakeholders, the subjects of the first few meetings may be quite technical, so the invitation should include only the IT teams, initially. But, because everyone is typically included, they invited the other teams as optional attendees.

The AoCs finished the draft and got Maverick and Barker to allow Rabbit to organise the CoP.

**

A short time later into the DevOps journey, users from across the organisation joined the first DevOps Community Meetup (which would become the catalyst to a CoP and other learning events such as dojos, lunch & learn chats, and various events started and driven by the volunteer CoP participants themselves).

Since it was the first Community Meetup, Maverick wanted to make it a big event. He and Barker stood in front of a packed auditorium, excited to see almost everyone from IT and a few users from the business.

Maverick cleared his throat and roared, *"Welcome to our first DevOps Community Meetup! We want to enable everyone to discuss and learn about all topics that support the DevOps mindset Barker, the DevOps team, the AoCs and I have launched over the last few months.*

"We have seen results, some great and some less than great, as we moved to a more Agile way of working. For a number of you, this has been disruptive to your normal processes. This Meetup is for active engagement and feedback; a place to share what is and is not working.

"Leadership wants to ensure that we are on target for our agreed upon corporate goals via IT strategies that influence our digital

transformation, appetite for success, and the intrinsic quest for built-in quality. With that, Agent 9, the stage is yours!"

Agent 9 took his place on the stage, ready to kick things off.

"Welcome! This is our first Meetup, and we really appreciate your active participation and candid feedback!

"We have placed a pen and pack of sticky notes under your seat. Use them to make notes or add questions to the parking lot at each station in the back of the auditorium where one of the AoCs or DevOps team members will be presenting and discussing one of these topics:

1. ***Continuous Integration,*** *which is enabled by code repositories and good version control practises.*
2. ***Continuous Delivery,*** *where you will find out more about moving your code from build to deploy.*
3. ***Continuous Testing,*** *where we encourage test first principles and how to improve quality by shifting left while taking some of the hard work out of manual testing.*
4. ***Configuration as Code,*** *where we will learn some very cool techniques used by DevOps gurus to automate and improve configuration management for our resources.*

"After each group moves through the four stations, we will then take a 15-minute break before coming back together to discuss the last subject, ***Unified Pipelines,*** *which connects all four station topics together. Enjoy and learn. See you all at the 60-minute break!"*

Continuous Integration (CI)

Agent 13 opened his presentation on Continuous Integration by explaining the good practise of sharing code, using a shared version control repository.

"Before we can integrate our work and workflow, using modern development techniques, a modern code repository is key. We

encourage everyone to store all your code in a shared version control repository and adopt a proven branching strategy, such as GitFlow (Driessen, Vincent, 2010) *or* Trunk-based development (Hammant, Paul, 2017-2018).

"Using these suggested techniques helps isolate code changes in feature branches and merge changes back to your single-source-of-truth, 'trunk' or 'master branch'. This avoids many potential merge conflicts and hunting for errors or the source of conflicts and other quality issues."

The group listened intently, the developers and engineers taking notes quickly.

Agent 13 continued, *"The DevOps team is using the modern Git version control repository, which allows us to submit a Pull Request* (Microsoft, 2018) *to trigger an optional validation build and a transparent review of and collaboration on changes. Once approved, changes are merged into the target branch, which prompts the continuous integration build. With this simple workflow, we promote pair programming, collaboration, and quality. Like magic!"*

Agent 13 then addressed the first parking lot question: **Can we automate and move jobs, such as vulnerability and code complexity scans, to the Pull Request validations?**

"Good question," he said. *"Notice on this diagram (Figure 20) that, while we run the CI Script, other integration tasks also run, such as unit tests, security vulnerability, and code quality scans. This is the beauty of the continuous integration build that can save many headaches later by running, what we call, a CI Pipeline. Perhaps, the DevOps team could trigger the same build as part of the Pull Request validations, which, in turn, would run your scans."*

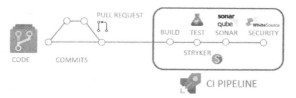

Figure 20 - Continuous Integration (CI) pipeline

"I really like this," one engineer commented. *"It allows us to shift left and empower developers to write better code, raise overall quality, and fail-fast as soon as possible."*

Another slide covered Continuous Integration.

Continuous Integration (CI) is the practise of building and confirming code changes continuously while automating manual tasks where possible.

Always:

- **Define branch policies** to enforce your desired quality criteria and support a healthy and always deployable master branch.
- **Minimise merge conflicts** with short-lived feature branches that isolate small and testable code changes. As shown in Figure 21, the longer your branches live, the greater the code drift and opportunity for conflict, which stifles productivity and review collaboration.
- **Commit Often** to support these two points and reduce changes of merge conflicts.

 AoCs do **not** encourage the use of text-heavy slides. The information enclosed in rectangles depicts speaker notes for visual slides with little to no text.

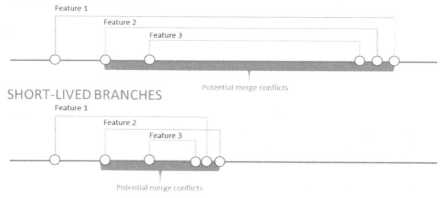

Figure 21 - Long versus Short-lived branches

- **Review the code changes** to confirm technical governance and encourage information transfers.
- **Maintain a consistent CI process,** which executes as fast as possible, otherwise your teams will revolt!

Do not rely only on the practise of continuous integration to trigger your build, test, security scan, or other validation engineering process. Complement CI with scheduled triggers (weekly, monthly) to pick up dependency and technology drift.

Continuous Delivery (CD)

At Station 2, Agent 77 briefed another group on Continuous Delivery. He also used slides, projecting onto his whiteboard.

*"Folks, **Continuous Delivery** (CD) is the process to build, test, configure and deploy a build artefact or potentially consumable feature. The successful continuous integration build triggers the continuous delivery process, which enables progressively longer-running activities, such as integration, load, system, and user acceptance testing. As you can see in the slide here on my monitor, starting with code, we do frequent commits after a pull request that trigger the CI pipeline after a series of automated tasks. This harmonious union is what we refer to a CI/CD pipeline (see Figure 22)."*

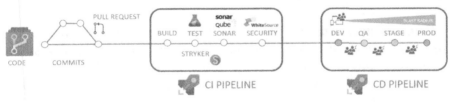

Figure 22 – Continuous Integration (CI) and Delivery (CD) pipeline

Umpty wrote a parking lot question: **Does CD not stand for continuous deployment?**

Agent 77 decided it was a good time to answer Umpty's question written on a large sticky note by discussing the next slide.

"There is a subtle difference between Continuous Delivery and Continuous Deployment. The latter deploys to a single environment, and every change goes directly to production. Continuous Delivery

deploys to several environments, such as development, QA, pre-production, and production, or sequences a few deployment rings to control the blast radius of change. You can explore deployment rings in the article, <u>Deploying New Releases: Feature flags or rings</u> (Agent 13, 2018).

"So, in our context and for our purpose, the team has agreed on continuous delivery as we are deploying to development, quality & assurance, and other non-production environments, which are located in the cloud," Agent 77 explained.

Continuous Testing (CT)

Agent 9 had the attention of his group at the neighboring station, teaching continuous testing.

*"**Continuous testing** is a method used to assess individual and integrated units of source code, data sets, and operating procedures against requirements to determine the quality and fit for use. By minimizing tests to save time and cost, you are deferring failure and defect resolution to later stages of your development process. The later we find and fix a bug, the greater the impact and cost.*

"There are many types of tests that help us embrace built-in quality. We will focus on six of them." He displayed his first slide.

- *unit*
- *integration*
- *system*
- *performance*
- *penetration*
- *regression testing*

 Boundless jumped in, *"Will we discuss mutation testing today?"*

"Unfortunately, we won't have time," Agent 9 replied. *"However, I recommend that you all read the* Mutation testing by example: Evolving from fragile TDD *article* (Bunardzic, Alex, 2019) *for information on that."*

Agent 9 showed several more screens, containing details on certain types of testing.

Unit tests (**Figure 23**) assess a small piece (unit) of code, typically limited to a handful of lines. They must be razor focused and fast, with no external dependencies.

"It's all in memory and typically combined with a test-driven-development (TDD) mindset," added Agent 9. *"With TDD, we test first, relying on continuous, short development cycles and tests that represent the requirements and software that is improved until we pass the test cases. Thus, we embrace failure, reflect, and adapt until all tests pass."*

Test First Development (TFD) is the first step in TDD and supports improved CI and CD as we approach our coding to fail until we pass. This improves quality as well and forms one of the options in our Test Strategy goal, using the decision and options chosen by the team.

Figure 23 - Unit Testing

Integration tests (**Figure 24**) assess different and integrated pieces of the system in its entirety or in parts. Due to potential for additional complexity and the fact that they are difficult means that IT and SITs (system integrated tests) are more expensive than unit tests. Integration tests need to be tested against any external dependencies, such as a database, a service, APIs or micro service, if a dependency exists.

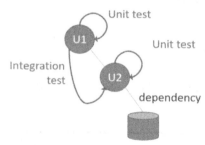

Figure 24 - Integration Testing

We call out SITs specifically from integration testing as they go beyond the integration unit tests and external dependencies.

System integration tests (**Figure 25**) assess a complete and integrated system, including requirements and standards compliance like System and Organisation Controls (SOC) examinations.

"This is very important since Big Corp works on software that has health and safety implications. Regulatory and legal compliance must be tested," Agent 9 correlated.

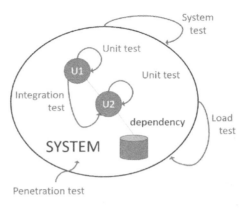

Figure 25 - System, Load, and Penetration Testing

Boundless left a question on Agent 9's parking lot: **Are these the only tests we need to worry about?**

"No, there are many testing strategies, goals decisions and options, which you may want to use depending on your situation. This is merely scratching the surface. There are many others that I have compiled on this slide," answered Agent 9, pointing to the screen.

User Experience tests are focused on determining how well users work with the product or solution, with the intention of finding areas for improvement. Users interact with the product, which is monitored or other feedback-looped, allowing discovery of how the product or feature can be improved. This is sometimes called usability or consumability testing.

Penetration tests assess the vulnerability of your system, using simulated cyberattacks. Mature organisations invest in rival red and blue teams. The blue team is trained to detect and oppose efforts by the red team in order to breach their system. The goal of the initiative is to detect vulnerabilities in both the system and organisation's culture while promoting the core value of validated learning and collaboration with different engineering teams.

Regression tests re-assess functional and non-functional tests after making changes to the system.

"Basically, with integration and delivery, testing needs to be continuous and automated wherever possible. It cannot be an afterthought or viewed as a tax that increases developer workload or bloats project cost and the project roadmap. Agent 13, who worked at Microsoft, said that their Azure DevOps Service build ran more than 70,000-unit tests at a rate of 10,000-unit tests per minute (Schaub, Willy-Peter, 2018). *So, it is doable!"*

Producing a **high quality** and **secure** solution is a must, especially with critical systems such as vehicles, health products, airplanes. It cannot be overstated. Would you board a ship you knew the engineers cut corners on and ignored built-in quality?

Automaton exclaimed, "*Love it. I can automate a lot, if not everything, in the continuous integration and delivery process.*"

Agent 9 chuckled, "*I suggest not trying automating everything at once. Rather, automate everything that is automatable over time. Remember, automation is not the goal; delivering value is!*"

Continuous, by definition, means that we continuously **observe**, **learn**, and **act**. With the DevOps mindset we foster Guided Continuous Improvement, collaborate and share, there are NO Silos! We should not sunset the accountability until we deprecate the last solution feature.

Are you doing something more than once? Are others repeating the task? Discuss whether this can be automated with your team then automate!

Configuration as Code

The AoCs brought in a configuration as code (CaC) specialist from the engineering department at Big Corp. She and Automaton were working on several projects where they could pilot CaC and Infrastructure as Code (IaC) with some new, on premise and cloud technologies. Automaton explained that CaC is the management of configuration for provisioned resources.

"You treat your configuration like code, which means you store configuration in a version control system and manage (and test) configuration changes with the same vigor as code changes.

"Configuration flows through your pipeline alongside your build artefacts. You deploy the same build with a unique configuration to every environment. If you must rebuild or re-deploy your solution to make configuration changes, you are not practising configuration as code," he cautioned.

A parking lot question asked: **What products can we use for configuration as code?**

Azure DevOps offers rich support for continuous integration (CI), continuous delivery (CD), extensibility, integration with open source and commercial off-the-shelve (COTS) software as a service (SaaS) solutions, such as Stryker, SonarQube, WhiteSource, Jenkins, and Octopus.

Many of the engineers and operations folks were impressed and excited that some DevOps mindset principles (people) along with processes and technologies were already being used with a positive impact. This was near and dear to Automaton's heart, and he was very interested in scripting, CaC, IaC and automation. However, he was prone to forget that products are only 5% of the journey.

 When practising configuration as code you should track and manage **configuration drift** caused by humans "turning knobs and dials," converting consistent environments into unique snowflakes. You need a process and solution to detect and remediate drift, preferably automatically, otherwise changes that people either do not know about or are buried deep in the CaC processes get lost and break things, which incidentally was part of the 2AM problem that raised so many issues and was difficult to triage. CaC is powerful just like IaC, however, with power comes responsibility.

Infrastructure as Code

Automaton's colleague spoke about Infrastructure as Code, which is the management and provisioning of infrastructure, such as cloud services, virtual machines and networks, and virtual resources.

Like CaC, you describe your infrastructure with the same vigor as code and automate the provisioning as part of your CD pipeline. You should also track and manage infrastructure drift as well to avoid unexpected costs such as provisioning memory, storage or compute resources unexpectedly or accidentally de-provision a critical resource.

"I believe if you embrace CaC and IaC, you can automate and deliver consistent and stable environments continuously, rapidly, and at scale with confidence," remarked Automaton.

 Azure DevOps Anti Drift (ALM DevOps Rangers, 2020) - A tool to detect and remediate drift between team projects in Azure DevOps.

Both Barker and Maverick were duly impressed. Their staff was clearly enjoying the DevOps Community Meetup. They heard laughter and many side conversations throughout the hour.

They regrouped after the fourth station to learn about what tied it all together.

A Unified CI/CD Pipeline

While Agent 13 flipped through his deck of slides in search of Figure 26, Agents 9 and 77 perused and photographed the parking lots to add make sure they had not missed any questions and responded to anyone with remaining questions or those requiring more research or clarification.

"Now that all of you have had a chance to get a brief introduction to Continuous Integration, Deployment, Testing and some of the processes and tools that support Configuration and Infrastructure as Code; it is time to connect the pipe in a way that is manageable and sustainable. Let us discuss how we can streamline our CI/CD pipeline to stabilize infrastructure environments, optimise flow, and create consistent, repeatable, and automated tasks.

"We want to enable our Service Reliability Engineers (SRE), turn complex into complicated tasks, as outlined by the Cynefin Sensemaking model *(Snowden, Dave, 1999), reduce maintenance cost and increase quality, consistency, and reliability,"* Agent 13 began.

"Typically, the biggest challenge is breaking down one or more processes based on decades of rules, regulations, and areas of comfort. If there is no balance between the development team's autonomy *and the organisation's* technical governance*, you will end up with a diversity of fragmented and duplicated CI/CD pipelines."*

He clicked through each slide while speaking to what was presented.

Find a **common ground** between development teams, driving speedboats wanting to access everything, iterate continuously, enable users, and release continuously and fast and operations folks, driving sluggish super tankers through the release with precision and patience.

Operations favours consistency, control and keeping the lights on with quality. This is understandable as they are usually the first called when there is a problem. Thus, some operations folks would prefer to enact measures to lock down change under the illusion that it protects the business and users.

Promoting process, standards, and governance that are hard to automate results in slower than expected release cycles and does not give flexibility for change. In fact, this is the reason why we have a DevDev mindset rather than a DevOps. It causes silos between development and engineering and operations.

You could hear a pin drop as everyone eagerly tried to process the tsunami of what this meant and the change in behaviour that needed to take place to make DevOps work.

At this point, Barker looked at Maverick who turned to the AoCs.

"The AoCs are correct. We need to change this behaviour and work together as one team even across our projects. This is why it is called DevOps!" Maverick declared.

Barker initiated clapping and most everyone followed suit, some reluctantly.

Agent 13 interrupted the applause to elaborate. *"As shown in Figure 26, we advocate a few principles that enable one unified pipeline per product.*
- *Start and end value with the customer*
- *Automate everything automatable*
- *Build with the aim to do it once*
- *Continuously integrate and deliver*

- *Continuously streamline and look for ways to improve*
- *Maintain one build definition*
- *Maintain one release pipeline definition*
- *Scan for vulnerabilities early and often to find failures fast*
- *Test first, early and often, failing as fast as possible*
- *Measure traceability and observability of the releases often"*

He moved to the next slide and said.

Keep it simple! If you cannot explain the reason (WHAT, WHY) and the process (HOW) of your pipeline, you likely do not understand your engineering process and are potentially contributing to technical debt. Ask yourself, 'What value is this providing?'

Agent 13 continued. *"We do not need an ultramodern and revolutionary pipeline, just one that is functional, valuable, and enabling for engineering, making the expected value happen faster and safer, resulting in delighted stakeholders,"* he supplemented before moving ahead with the presentation.

*"Good practise encourages **one** CI/CD pipeline with **one** build definition per application used to trigger pull request, pre-merge validation and continuous integration builds."*

Many in the audience had begun taking notes, creating new question post-it notes and listening intently to the many ideas, concepts and deep topics.

Agent 13 gained momentum as he waded deeper into his element on this subject.

"Generate a release build with debug information *and upload to the symbol server. This enables developers to debug locally by remoting into production without having to worry about which build or retrieve symbols from the symbol server,"* he carried on enthusiastically, showing more slides that expounded on his guidance.

The slide covered:

> **SHIFT-LEFT!** Perform as many validations as possible in the build, allowing feature teams to fail-fast, continuously raise overall product quality, and include invaluable evidence with every pull request for the reviewers.

Many in the room understood that Shift-Left meant doing some technical modeling or even hard work up front to meet costs, drastically reducing risk and other expensive factors. Additionally, doing so improved the reliability of the project, making it less prone to fail, exceed budgets or disappoint.

"Do you prefer a pull request with a gazillion commits or one with minimal commits and supporting evidence, such as security vulnerabilities, test coverage, code quality, and Stryker mutant remnants?" he posed to the audience, pausing only briefly before exclaiming, *"I do not know about you, but I vote for the latter!"*

Several nodded, remembering his instruction about code repositories and committing code often along with the article on Mutation Testing he cited as a resource.

*"**Avoid build transformation,** generating multiple environment specific builds. Create **one** build and perform release-time transformation, tokenization, and/or XML/JSON value replacement. In other words, SHIFT-RIGHT environment configuration,"* he continued.

*"**Securely store release configuration data,** making it available to both the DEV and OPS teams, based on the level of trust and sensitivity of the data. Consider the open source Key Manager, Azure Key Vault, AWS Key Management Service (AWS KMS), or one of many other products – there are many tools for your toolkit!"* he exclaimed.

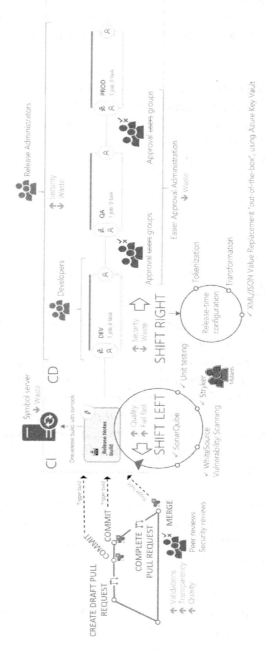

Figure 26 - Unified Pipeline

*"We should **use groups** rather than users. Instead of duplicating pipelines to give teams access to their areas of interest, create one pipeline and grant access to specific stages of the delivery environments.*

*"Lastly, **embrace pull requests** to help raise insight and transparency into your codebase, increase the overall quality, improve collaboration, and release pre-validation builds into selected environments like DEV."* He finished presenting, scanning the attentive audience for questions or concerns.

"But aren't we already doing all this!?!" Wiggle exclaimed, looking uncertain.

Boundless rolled his eyes and stood up and said, *"Wiggle, we may **think** we are already doing it all, but only some of us use pipelines. In fact, much of what we do is not automated, and we do not use CI much at all. If you take the time to explore the variety of choices and tools available in DevOps, you will see that we are nowhere near a unified pipeline. Given we have several pilot pipelines, disabled testing for some project, uncovered code, a pile of technical debt and bugs, you will realise that keeping it SIMPLE and CONSISTENT has never been our focus,"* he disclosed and remained standing.

"Good point, Boundless," Maverick commended. *"Let's regroup after today's session and discuss how we can audit our environments to determine where we are aligned with the AoCs' recommendations."*

"Right, this is a good place pause," Agent 9 took a deep breath. *"We covered **a lot** of technical territory today. Maverick has provided lunch and, when we regroup for the afternoon session, more business users will join us for the final topic."*

Selecting the Right DevOps Boat (Project)

While everyone lined up for the buffet of sandwiches, salads, and other goodies, Maverick, Barker, and Redline took the opportunity to continue their previous discussion on selecting a project to become the pilot for the DevOps program.

Barker flipped open his laptop and shared his updated and prioritised product backlog. *"See, Maverick? These are the work items we have discussed."*

Everyone noticed a post-it note at the bottom of backlog with 'Due in 8 weeks' written on it. Redline sighed as she reviewed the long and daunting list of work items and unfinished stories. She had not been invited to the backlog discussion, even though she had been promoted from web developer to the Team Lead (**Scrum Master**) for the pilot project.

"Which stories are the most important?" she asked.

"They are all important!" Maverick retorted.

At that moment, Barker recalled a conversation he and Redline had with Agent 77 about **Risk - Value prioritization** and realised that Redline should have been part of his backlog discussion with Maverick. Instead, he over-committed, potentially dooming the entire team.

Barker could see he missed the opportunity to explain these points to Maverick and gave a consoling look to Redline, who simply bowed her head and said, *"I see ..."*

Redline hid her facial expression because she was becoming agitated. As a doer, not a talker, she wanted to get things done, experimenting and pivoting as needed. Getting a predefined menu with deadlines was not her cup of tea.

"Well," she sighed. *"I can already visualise Umpty, representing Quality assurance and testing for this pilot, stressing more than usual."*

Barker got up to stand in the buffet line.

"Let me review with you and Maverick which key stories are the least risky and likely to deliver the most value. This may mean that not all of these need to be done by this timeline," he offered.

This made Redline relax a little. *"That would be great! Then let us get the team together for details and any clarifications and begin mapping the stories for the first iteration."* She felt re-energised with a sense of direction.

Maverick informed, *"The first set of work items are definitely priority one, so I suggest Barker and the team get moving on them."*

"In the meantime, I will ask the team to categorize the items that seem most complex and those that appear simple, using coloured sticky notes - red for complex, blue for medium difficulty and green for simple," she suggested to Barker, who liked the idea of colour coding so much that he became slightly annoyed that he did not think of it himself.

Old behaviours die-hard for IT managers used to the command and control style. Thus, it may be a while before he realises that the DevOps mindset encourages transparent communication, and there is no **me**, **myself**, or **I** in a self-organising, self-managing team.

Invite the Business to the CoP

Agent 9 reconvened the Meetup after lunch, greeting all the Scrum Masters, product owners and other business stakeholders.

"We covered a lot of fairly technical, essential practises of the common engineering system this morning. To complement this

beyond just delivering, we need to discuss two more key concepts in achieving continuous delivery of value," he informed, giving the stage to Agents 13 and 77.

"Welcome to the most important aspect of why we do what we do; the customer!" Agent 13 projected the first slide onto the screen while Agent 77 continued.

"As we have previously mentioned, value must start and end with the customer. We introduced value streams and the need to execute value as fast as possible, showing that lost time and delayed release means a loss, period.

"Thus, the need to gain speed and bring value quickly relies heavily on feedback and minimizing waste," Agent 77 referenced the screen that echoed his words.

> **Lean principles** drive results for achieving value quickly, effectively and efficiently, using a minimum business increment (MBI), which works best with things that are known.

"Agent 13 will discuss unknown things," he relayed, handing Agent 13 the slide clicker.

*"Two excellent ways to bring knowns from the unknowns and speed your delivery of value are **hypothesis driven development** and **vertical slicing**. Both are practises that thrive on small, tangible Feature increments. The days of monolithic black boxes are over!"* he exclaimed, revealing his first slide.

Hypothesis Driven Development

"Traditional or Waterfall delivery gave us a potentially predictable and process-driven delivery practise that, many times, turned out to be an illusion as no delivery is completely predictable. Figure 27, as we see on the screen, shows the time and effort invested to deliver a quality set of Features after hiding behind closed doors for a long period.

"At the time of delivery, our solution was often outdated and our patient users disappointed. Agile enabled us to create and respond to change more quickly by delivering working software, then sensing, learning, and responding." Agent 13 scanned the audience to ensure he had allowed enough time to absorb the diagram before moving to the next slide.

Figure 27 - Traditional delivery

"Figure 28 illustrates three releases, X.1, X.2, and X.3, using Agile delivery methods. After release X.1, we improve feature 3 based on user feedback and re-deploy the feature in release X.3. This is a simple example of delivering features more often while remaining focused on working software in response to user feedback."

Figure 28 - Agile-style delivery

Both AoCs were careful to gauge the audience's attention and comprehension as the presentation progressed, ready to pause if necessary. The sea of eyes, focused on the stage, signaled them to resume.

"Managing this with the right control means measuring effectively," Agent 77 said, introducing the next segment.

Manage Your Blast Radius of Change

Agent 13 cued up the next slide, reviewing the bulleted items and citing the article, <u>Deploying new releases: Feature flags or rings</u> (Agent 13, 2018) for reference.

He explained, *"A Feature Flag allows us to create a function or feature in our product, which is a useful DevOps technique. When we add Feature Flags to our release flow* Figure 29, *we can toggle features ON (enabled and exposed) or OFF (disabled and hidden).*

"In this example, Feature Flags for features 2, and 6 are OFF. Although the features are deployed to production, they are not exposed to the user. We can fine-tune the features (value) of each release, after deploying to production, which is very powerful and efficient.

"If your development and engineering teams are able to build two features when the business is unsure which is better, one can be hidden but available at a flick of a switch. This is economic for our DevOps team while also being controllable by the business, and it facilitates feedback from our customer or user, allowing us to determine (with a toggle) if that Feature is providing more or less value," Agent 13 took a sip of water and scanned his notes before proceeding.

Figure 29 – Feature Flag-style delivery

"Controlling and managing our releases is also important, whether due to business, legal or other reasons. Ring-based deployment helps in these cases," Agent 13 appended.

 Separating delivery from release enables us to release on demand, controlled by the business, not IT!

Exposing features in the canary and early-adopter rings allows us to evaluate without the risk of an all-or-nothing, big-bang deployment, as shown in **Figure 30**.

Feature Flags decouple release deployment and feature exposure. As shown in **Figure 31**, you "flip the flag" to expose or hide a new feature, perform an emergency rollback or allow users to toggle preview.

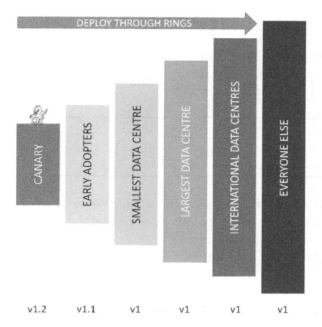

Figure 30 – Blast Radius

Figure 31 – Feature Flag launch panel

 When you combine deployment rings and Feature Flags, you can progressively deploy a release through rings, using Feature Flags to fine-tune the deployed release.

Add Hypothesis-Driven Development

The next presentation section appeared, so the AoCs took a moment to allow everyone to finish taking their notes and reset in preparation for the next wave of information.

> Hypothesis-Driven Development is based on a series of experiments to confirm or disprove a hypothesis in a complex problem domain where we have **unknown - unknowns**.

"This is what Agent 77 was talking about; when we are not sure about our product or feature and need to find out how much value, if any, or if the product will function correctly," Agent 13 added, linking the concept to a previous discussion for the audience's benefit.

"Some of you may have heard of the Lean Startup by Eric Ries. One of the Agile lifecycles that fits nicely here is the exploratory Lean lifecycle explained in 'Choose your WoW'.

"Your DevOps team can work with known and unknown projects, using different Agile lifecycles, which allows the business and IT teams to choose HOW they work instead of via prescribed, pre-defined processes and dates," Agent 13 explained.

The audience looked astonished at the mention of no pre-defined or forced processes and no pre-defined dates for release. A murmur began, as they talked amongst themselves about such an option!

Agent 13 hushed the crowd by maintaining focus and pace.

"We want to find practical ideas or fail fast. Instead of developing a monolithic solution and performing a big-bang release, we iterate through hypotheses, evaluating how features perform and, most importantly, how and if customers use them."

Barker stood up and asked, *"Do you have a blueprint on how we should be defining our experiments?"*

"Yes, a simple template to use is on the next slide."

> **We believe** {customer/business segment} **wants**
> {product/feature/service} **because** {value prop}.

"Using that statement, we can craft our first example," he said,
showing the next slide that contained the populated formula.

> **We believe** that users **want** to be able to select different themes
> **because** it will result in improved user satisfaction. We expect 50%
> or more users to select a non-default theme and a 5% increase in user
> engagement.

*"Remember that every experiment must be based on a hypothesis
with a measurable conclusion while contributing to the feature and
overall product learning,"* Agent 13 reminded.

"Consider these steps for each experiment:

1. *Observe your user.*
2. *Define a hypothesis and an experiment to assess it.*
3. *Define clear success criteria, such as a 5% increase in user
   engagement.*
4. *Run the experiment.*
5. *Evaluate the results and either accept or reject the hypothesis.*
6. *Repeat these steps."*

"Thank you," said Barker. *"I think we have a quite bit of
refactoring work to do on our backlog."* He blushed, sitting back
down to make a note to do so.

Agent 13 flipped to his final slide.

*"When we deploy each release, we can see user behaviour and
feedback and approve or disprove the hypothesis that motivated the
deployment. As shown in Figure 32, the experiment for features 2
and 6 fails. We can fail-fast by removing those features from the*

release and avoid carrying waste that is not delivering value or delighting our users!

"Notice on this slide that the experiments for feature 3 is inconclusive, so we adapt the feature, the experiment, and perform A|B testing in Release X.2. Based on observations, we find the variant feature 3.2 is the winner and re-deploy in release X.3. We only expose the features that passed the experiment and satisfied the users," Agent 13 finished, feeling confident about the overall value of the Meetup.

Figure 32 - Hypotheses driven development with Feature Flags

Light Up Progressive Exposure

When a hypothesis-driven development is combined with progressive exposure strategies, we can vertically slice our solution, incrementally delivering on our long-term vision over minimum business increments. This translates into confirmed value or no value very quickly. Knowing that there is no value is still valuable when done early in the project.

 Embracing hypothesis driven development supports the empirical process theory and its three pillars of **transparency**, **inspection**, and **adaption**.

Agent 77 displayed their Wiki page on the large screen. The AoCs then took turns, reading the highlights of the presentation.

Hypothesis-driven development

- Contains a series of experiments to confirm or disprove a hypothesis (fail fast) – finding value!
- Delivers a measurable conclusion and enables continued learning.
- Enables continuous feedback from stakeholders and users - understanding the unknown – unknowns!
- Allows us to understand the evolving landscape into which we progressively expose value.

Progressive Exposure:

- Is not an excuse to hide non-production ready code. **Always ship production-ready quality**!
- Deploys a release of features through rings in production. **Limit blast radius**!
- Enables or disables features in production. **Fine tune release values**!
- Relies on patterns, such as circuit breakers, to protect the infrastructure from implications of progressive exposure. **Observe, sense, act** (fail fast)!"

Although the AoCs granted a 15-minute break between sessions, no one left the auditorium except for a few engineers. The open and vibrant discussions were a refreshing change to the traditional sit-down-and-listen sessions the AoCs often attended.

A Vertical Slice to Accelerate Business Value

Agent 77 opened the last stretch of the long, informative day with a bulleted summary of talking points from the previous sessions.

- Discussed key tools and strategies to support delivering business value faster
- Introduced Minimum Business Increments (MBIs)

> - Determined that delivering a product or Feature, regardless of when, makes it potentially consumable.
> - So, we only release functional, ready to be used software or products.

"Now, we will explore Vertical Slicing," he announced, moving to a slide with its definition.

> A Vertical Slice (VS) is a top to bottom, fully implemented and tested piece of functionality that provides some form of business value to an end user – (Ambler, Scott, 2012-2015).

"Do you have examples of when and why we should use vertical slicing?" Barker asked.

"Sure do!" said the AoCs as Agent 77 displayed a Glossary and concise list from their Wiki.

> Use vertical slicing when:
>
> 1. Focusing on a single, small piece of work to expose a feature found earlier in your Agile process as high value and manageable risk.
> 2. Breaking up complex and/or large pieces of functionality into more manageable, less risky and faster sections.
> 3. It is unclear from the stakeholders how much or how little value a feature or function might deliver. VS can measure feedback easier and earlier so a change in course can occur and steer the team faster.
> 4. Working on complex solutions like Data Warehouse and Business Intelligence (DWBI) projects with long cycles. VS can focus the data architects and experts on specific elements for the VS feature rather than taking a broader approach across the entire solution. Multiple "short" steps of work can be done while still maintaining a consistent and strategic intent of the DWBI solution.

"Okay..." Barker said, fading out with uncertainty. *"I am mulling over my backlog and, well, how exactly do I do this?"*

Agent 77 raised his eyebrows, suggesting the complexity of that question. *"Given the time we have remaining, answering that is not possible in this session. At least not answering it sufficiently,"* he clarified. *"However,"* he added. *"Under 'In Practise' on the Wiki, you will find more details. Here it is as well,"* he offered, presenting the information on the screen.

Vertical slicing can be performed:

- After the backlog stories have been prioritised for value / risk, etc.
- Once you begin detailing your work items on a set of features within the story mapping exercise.
- When you detail the HOW of each story, including your estimating exercises.

Barker thanked him for the resource and planned to follow up on it later. He knew the presentation needed to resume in order to finish on time.

The AoCs delved a bit deeper into Vertical Slicing before the Meetup timeslot came to its end.

"That concludes today's DevOps Community Meetup, and we thank you for attending the first event," Agent 9 expressed for the AoCs.

The audience applauded while Barker and Maverick shook hands over a successful event. Barker gestured for the AoCs to stay behind to quickly assess the Meetup, anxious to hear their feedback.

Failure, a Misunderstood Enabler

Once the auditorium had emptied, Barker questioned the consistent reference to embracing failure.

"I heard terms, like fail-fast, and, honestly, it made me uncomfortable. I'm uneasy with failure. Can we use a less poignant word to avoid ruffling Maverick or the Overlords' feathers?" he asked, almost pleadingly.

Agent 13 frowned. *"Oh dear, we have touched another nerve by poking at the need to embrace failure. Why do you think it is hard to accept failures as normal and an opportunity to learn?"* he pondered, waiting for Barker to do the same.

"In order to be successful, we need to desensitize the leadership to failure and elaborate on the value of embracing it. The fear of failure is rife in many organisations, including those on a digital transformation journey," Agent 13 reasoned. *"This is strange because when we look at the Manifesto for Agile Development, we notice references to customer **collaboration** and response to **change**.*

*"Lean thinking promotes principles, such as **optimize the whole, eliminate waste, create knowledge, build quality in,** and **respect people**. Lastly, two Kanban principles mention **visualize work** and **continuous improvement,** all of which involve failure and learning from it,"* he remarked.

Agent 13 then selected a section on the Wiki on fail-fast, succeed quicker, bringing it up on the projector screen.

"We believe an organisation will embrace failure if we elaborate on its benefit in the context of software engineering to all stakeholders," he informed. *"If we look at the traditional software development lifecycle again, we see that it strives for quality and is very sensitive to failure.*

"As shown in Figure 33, *we design, develop, and test all features using a strict process. The solution is released to the customer when QA and Security give us the 'thumbs up', which results in a happy (success) or unhappy (failure) user."*

Figure 33 – Traditional software development lifecycle

"A key distinction," Agent 9 inserted, *"is that only having **one** opportunity to fail or succeed can be an effective model when building a sensitive product, like a multi-million rocket or aircraft. So, context is important as well!"*

Agent 13 scrolled to another area on the Wiki.

"Here, in Figure 34, *we are shown more modern software development lifecycle that strives for quality and embraces failure. We design, build, test, and deliver a release with limited features to our users for preview, receiving immediate feedback. If the user is happy (success), we move to the next feature. If user is unhappy (failure), we either improve or scrap the feature based on the validated feedback."*

Figure 34 – Modern software development lifecycle

He gave Barker time to study the diagram.

*"Note that we have a **minimum** of **one** opportunity to fail per feature, giving us at least ten opportunities to improve our product, based on validated user feedback, before we release the same product. This modern approach is a repetition of the traditional approach, broken down into smaller release cycles. We cannot reduce the effort to design, develop, and test our features, but we <u>can</u> learn and improve the process,"* Agent 13 distinguished.

Agent 77 eagerly jumped into the discussion to clarify.

"We are not suggesting that teams fail or make mistakes on purpose. We simply mean that failure, when it occurs, should be embraced, creating a safe environment for teams to innovate and continuously learn. This allows us to succeed more quickly," he stopped, discouraged by Barker's facial expression, which suggested a combination of resistance and confusion. *"Look at it this way,"* he said, switching gears. *"Slowly failing is the epitome of failure, wasted time and money and risk. Therefore, failing slow is big failure, and the lessons learned are much more painful."*

Barker considered this.

"I think I get it now. So, smaller chunks of work, MBIs and vertical slicing mean failing is less risky, allowing us to move ahead with development or a hypothesis, which gives us the ability to deliver value quickly and reliably," he summarised, hoping for accuracy.

The AoCs exchanged glances then smiled; Barker got it! To be sure, Agent 13 reiterated the proper takeaways.

"When we fail, the waste and impact must be minimised and the validated learning maximized. To avoid the fear of failure amongst engineers, all stakeholders in an organisation need to trust the engineering process and allow failure to occur by planning, prioritising, building, releasing, and supporting with a common mindset. This is very different from suggesting that teams work recklessly or be oblivious to the impact of failure, especially when it affects investors or livelihoods."

Barker laughed and said, *"You are convincing, as usual. You guys certainly know a lot, and I am impressed."*

Agent 77 looked at his colleagues and laughed, *"I wish we could claim all of this as our own ideas, but much of it is from studying others' theories, concepts, books and leadership. Together, we strive to see what works and fits while measuring, adapting, growing and sharing, making us more like sharers of great ideas with practical knowledge and experience,"* he humbly explained.

Agent 13 recalled a motivating quote.

"You cannot be petrified of failure when developing software, otherwise you will stifle innovation and evolution, which, in turn, suffocates 'the union of people, process, and products to enable continuous delivery of value to our end users' (Donovan Brown, 2015).*"*

Before their brains could explode, they decided to call it a day, leaving the auditorium to Rabbit, who ran around, collecting sticky notes and a few leftovers.

The Boat Atmosphere Gets Heated

The DevOps team determined that it was time to kick-start the pilot project. Although Maverick and Barker had not decided exactly what the project software delivery would be, the team had an idea. In fact, Redline had seen Barker's backlog and timelines and had already told the team about the expectations within, which were going sky high!

Automaton made all sorts of whirling noises as he computed a low chance of success before an agreed set of stories, estimation and other work had occurred.

"If we are going to get this done in 8 weeks, we need to automate using continuous integration," he declared.

Knight, always the hero ready for action, had been working with Automaton and other engineers on potential pipelines with CI and CD. He chose to move the project forward.

"Yes," he agreed. *"Let us get our pipeline and scripts working, so we can start pushing the code into our build and test environments."*

Wiggle, on the other hand, was not thrilled about trying new things and had yet to be sold on the DevOps transformation.

"Woah, slow down!" she warned. *"We do not know enough about TDF or TDD to proceed using either, and we certainly don't have time to learn then deliver!"*

The QA testers and rest of the team shook their heads in concern.

Knight shrugged, confident as ever, exclaiming, *"We just heard from the AoCs that TDD is a journey. We will start with the Test First aspect of TDD and test before we refactor."*

"I set up a script, so we can pull our code from GIT and test it in our developer's environment, validate that it functions, push a button, and test it again before it commits back in GIT," boasted Automaton with his lights all flashing.

Everyone seemed confused. Not many developers or engineers used GIT since others, such as QA, provided testing after the code was written.

"We need to start using GIT. This is where we are going to store our code," Automaton urged. *"Remember, the repository...."*

Everyone nodded but had no idea what was needed. They began to worry about training, licenses, and anything else that may be required to get started.

"You mean we can do testing with this script before seeing the compiled code and running a whole bunch of tests to ensure the other developers do not break it?" Umpty asked in disbelief.

"You bet!" replied Boundless and Automaton in unison.

"That is exactly the point of the CI and, eventually, CD! Were you not paying attention at the Meetup today?" scoffed Knight.

"If they follow the rules...," Boundless thought to himself, having spent the past weekend confirming some testing and automation between pulling and committing code, reducing his concerns of developers breaking each other's code.

"Do not worry, everyone. Umpty, you and I will kick off a code Kata this week to show everyone how to use GIT, test and deploy. Then, we will see the pipeline in action by automating this in each of the environments - development, QA, pre-production, etc.," proposed Boundless, taking initiative.

The team got excited, especially the testers, who always had to wait before exploring, reviewing, and testing new code and environments. This could save everyone a lot of time!

Umpty looked down. He was still uncertain, mumbling, *"I'm not convinced that automation, TDD, or any the other wizardry we discuss will help us build better software, quicker."*

Everyone ignored his concern and gathered around a whiteboard, vibrantly discussing how long it would take to automate, learn TFD or TDD, and the stories Redline had seen in Barker's backlog.

When you face relentless resistance to change, switch into partisan mode, lead by example, educate by sharing, not talking.

"Let the dogs (critics) bark, as the caravan (change) passes."

DevOps Mindset Value 3 Goal Reached

Well done, we have reached our third goal: **Inspire and share collaboratively** instead of becoming a hero or silo. *No new silos to break down silos.*

Silos and DevOps are incompatible. All too often, an IT director brings in so-called DevOps experts who do not help Mindset Value 3 become attainable. Ignoring this goal only adds another silo to an already silo-riddled IT department and business. Creating "DevOps teams and titles" also goes against the very principles of Agile and DevOps, which are based on the concept of breaking down silos. In both Agile and DevOps, teamwork is essential, and if you do not work in a self-organizing team, you are doing neither of them. One way to really make this goal realised is through a community of practise, a strategy to bring the disparate business units together, share information, collaborate, and break down the walls that create siloed teams.

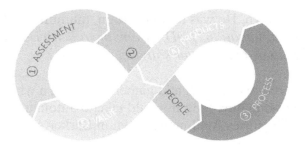

We can all **inspire** and **share collaboratively** instead of becoming a hero or creating a silo.

The Dock

After the successful CoP Meetup, the AoCs went back to the Dock to debrief and relax.

They sensed storms on the horizon, but a chance for a red sky at night (sailor's delight). They discussed the organisation's insightful **assessment** and stormy **culture** shock that lead to its initial embrace of the need to balance autonomy with technical governance and nurture a common and streamlined engineering **process**.

The organisation was on the verge of moving from the **forming** to the **storming** stage (Tuckman, Bruce, 2019), which meant they were heading into stormy and turbulent waters, where people often test their boundaries of influence and relationship with other crew members, requiring expert coaching to form a team.

They reflected on the turbulent transformation journey and the rocks and sharks they met along the way.

We are here
- Create the team
- Identify goals

Turbulent times

Forming   Storming   Norming   Performing

Figure 35 – Forming. Adapted from Tuckman's Stages of Group Development

"People are familiar and comfortable with silos, whereas working collaboratively across teams takes discipline. This a mindset change. Duplicating work, being absent for critical conversations and working for two masters and/or multiple projects are some of the rocks that people hit when initially putting DevOps into practise," Agent 77 forewarned.

"I encountered a shark with Rabbit when she uttered the familiar statement, 'We are already doing that', when, in reality, it is far from accurate. A little digging shows that people don't really want to make the effort to change," he professed.

"The fear of failure is overpowering and will stifle innovation. We need trust, lively debate, and an appetite for experimentation to streamline the engineering process effectively," Agent 13 affirmed.

Agent 9 agreed with his colleagues.

*"Many 'DevOps theorists' don't realise that they are **unconsciously incompetent** about their organisation's DevOps maturity. They would do their organisations a big favour if they tried to reach a **conscious incompetence** stage, at least,"* Agent 9 proclaimed.

Boat Inspection

A Monofunctional Lone Warrior Silo

Agent 77 remained at the office after hours to observe and chat with a project team that caught his attention. He pondered the **people:process:product** discussions with Barker and other managers, finding no rational reason why they insisted on working in silos while openly agreeing to collaboration.

Are they concerned for their position, power, influence, or need to control their own freedom? he wondered aloud.

The company was at a pivotal point where IT needed to shape up or ship out, yet there was resistance to working cooperatively and less competitively.

It was possible that some were genuinely concerned about their job and did not feel safe, sharing resources and working in an effective team. What concerned Agent 77 the most was that if there was a leak in the boat during a storm, it would take everyone working as a team, looking out for one another, to have any chance of survival.

In DevOps there are no silos. A "special DevOps team" that does not grow into a T-shaped feature or core team will eventually fail, missing the value they could bring to the whole organisation.
Silo teams are an anti-pattern.

Barker's team, with each member having a singular responsibility rather than a role, is made up of silos. Rabbit builds unit tests while Redline runs load tests. Umpty validates security and Wiggle owns the infrastructure. Team members defend their responsibilities and skills, never asking for help or stepping out of their comfort zone to help someone else. It is a landscape of passionate yet separate and isolated silos, which is a doomed work model.

"OK, I'm done. I'll lob it over the wall to the next silo and focus on my next task," is not the DevOps mindset, even if you use a Kanban board!

Agent 77 expressed his thoughts to Agent 9, who listened and shared his concerns.

"Business, development and operations must have a shared goal! Development and operations must be comfortable enough to pair and share responsibilities! They need to break down the silos into teams of collaborating engineers!" Agent 9 added, thoughtfully.

Agent 77 agreed that, although a siloed team can cope with unforeseen events and take responsibility for tasks that require an owner or other backing, it is neither a scalable nor encouraging environment.

"Cross-functional is a key part of genetic information for an effective team blueprint. Contrary to common belief, it does not imply that everyone in the team can do everything." - (Agent 13, 2018)

Encourage business, operational and development engineers to **collaborate**. Development engineers must understand, taking operations seriously and **ownership** of features in production until they are deprecated. The **team** owns releases and features, not an individual, business, development or operations.

Act 4

STORM - Building a Better Boat

Yet Another Morning Chat

"We must take the current when it serves or lose our ventures."
– William Shakespeare

After a few stormy days, the Agents of Chaos were tired but excited to have observed teams, making progress with their transformation journey. A breeze of exhilaration was sweeping through the organisation!

"Agents, I like how the Dock is coming along! The visuals and boards are great! May I ask a quick question that has been keeping me up at night?" Boundless asked.

The AoCs welcomed him to sit with them as they drank fresh cups of coffee and prepared for the day.

Boundless, ever-energetic, reported how the DevOps pilot was going and how the team was growing. He remarked that Barker was getting requests from developers all over the IT department to join. Conversely, those from operations were showing up at the Daily Stand-up but not involved in any of the stories.

"I remember the presentation and class about effective teams you held. One of the topics was team size. Can you explain the best practise to me again? How can we influence management to help us get-up-and-go to smaller teams and agility?" solicited Boundless.

Agent 77 winced when he heard the phrase 'best practise', and the other AoCs knew what would follow.

"If I may, Boundless," Agent 77 began. *"First, context counts, as a colleague always reminds me. Every situation is unique, depending on many scaling factors and context. You should weigh what the ideal size is with your Product Owner and team."*

"That is very true. Context absolutely counts," Agent 13 concurred. *"However, everyone should first agree that efficient communication is necessary to encourage transparency, collaboration, using cross-functional teams and effective information sharing."*

Agent 77 started drawing on their whiteboard while Agent 13 explained the concept that adding more members adds complexity to communication, potentially adding more lags, management and waste.

Agent 13 described Agent 77's drawing.

"When we draw three dots for a 3-member team then draw a communication line between each, it shows a simple network. When we repeat the exercise with 4 then 5 or even 9 members, you will notice the number of communication lines rising from 3, 6, 10, to 36.

"Once you breach 5 members, the inherent communication complexity becomes unproductive and potentially wasteful. In the worst-case scenario, this can cause quality issues to creep in, such as misinformation."

Agent 9 scanned the whiteboard.

"Interesting," he remarked. *"If you replace team members with teams in your visual, it becomes evident that the number of connections and associated complexity is the same for communication between teams as it is for individual team members."*

"Great observation, Agent 9! This is one reason silos are born. Teams interact well within their own team, but the more they interact outside of their team, becoming reliant on others to support them, the harder things get," Agent 77 cautioned.

It is important to be mindful that transparent and cross-functional teams allow the flow of information freely, almost naturally, so that teams interact with each other as needed, when needed. Additionally, any stakeholder's ability to clearly, transparently and easily see what each team is doing and how the project is going is equally as important.

"Wow, this is a fantastic visual way to demonstrate the challenge of creating vibrant collaboration between all our teams and stakeholders," Boundless exclaimed, amazed at how easy it was to understand that large teams are linked, potentially ineffective teams.

After their discussion, the AoCs continued to discuss optimizing the pilot project way of working, using approaches in Scaled and Disciplined Agile. This approach of reviewing performance and roadblocks in the Retrospectives allowed the AoCs to encourage the Agile and DevOps teams to weather the adoption storm and continue to transform. This guided, continuous approach was a key differentiator to other Agile expert coaches, demonstrating velocity for their clients in their journey to innovate and improve.

Boat Becomes Creaky

Word was spreading across Big Corp. Maverick and Barker were talking to everyone about how much velocity their new DevOps team was creating. Many of the DevOps team members were also speaking to their colleagues, offering advice and expounding on the virtues of DevOps. Across IT, many requested to be part of the new DevOps team, even inquiring about the community of practise, which had just recently formed!

As work seemed to be completed faster, many great ideas emerged. Teams noticed their managers, opening up to experimentation, prompting members to search for ways to improve the process and product.

Barker maintained his dashboards and regular updates but not always as fast as he desired, so he continued to check in with the various teams, attending the stand ups and asking how things were progressing, being measured, and determined good enough to stop innovating and improving. He was very excited with the teams' speed of getting the demos out.

Barker arrived to attend a daily stand up that was about to start as the sprint was almost finished.

Redline, sitting with the DevOps project team, glanced around and noticed Barker observing. She and her team held their round table on what they worked on yesterday and planned to work on today. Redline asked if there were any issues stopping or blocking the team from being able to complete their stories or work items, listening to their quick responses that contained no obstacles.

She concluded the stand up, saying, *"Good stand up! We are finishing our first sprint, and tomorrow is the Retrospective!"* Redline smiled, everyone seemed happy except Barker, who appeared determined.

"Make sure you're able to make it to the Retrospective. It is particularly important we get everyone's feedback. The AoCs will be here to listen in on how things went on this sprint."

This caused some of the team members to become nervous. Not all the story points were finished because the team was unable to focus on one task as they were context switching due to their manager or others constantly interrupting and asking for help. Everyone on the team was also assigned to other projects in addition to the DevOps project, given an added workload without a discussion or plan to address the impacts to their other commitments.

Umpty nervously wondered, *"What if we need to say something that may be negative?"*

"Do not worry, Umpty. We are all in a safe room, so do not hold back from constructive comments and critical points," Redline assured.

Barker could tell his past command and control style still lingered, inciting fear in the team. Since beginning the transformation, however, he had started softening his approach.

"That's right," he confirmed. *"I promise not to put any names down to any points or suggestions unless told to. I also want all of you to be open about your feelings and concerns. I value your suggestions and promise not to penalize anyone, even if I don't agree!"* he pledged.

The whole team relaxed with that statement. Redline and Barker asked Automaton and Knight to stay after the stand-up to discuss the burn-down chart, which also needed updating. Everyone else was free to return to work with their clear expectations.

As the group disbursed, Maverick dashed into the room suddenly.

"Sorry to intrude!" he blurted breathlessly. *"Barker, I need a word please!"*

"Okay..." Barker straightened up, looking a tad concerned.

"We just got a call from infrastructure team, and a new vulnerability patch has to go out immediately!" Maverick demanded, unapologetically.

Barker became annoyed. The team was making serious progress, and he did not want to add a pivot or a problem to their plan.

"What?" he asked, impatiently. *"Can we not wait until tomorrow to look at this when we are done our sprint?"* Barker pleaded.

Maverick shook his head, knowing he was throwing a wrench into the DevOps project.

"No, absolutely not. You cannot ship your product until this patch goes out. Did you get the security team to sign off on your changes?" Maverick asked, directly.

Maverick already knew the answer but felt this was a problem Barker would just have to solve. Redline looked to Barker, who looked back to her. They silently acknowledged the need to tend to the patch and prepare the demo for tomorrow.

Maverick repeated the deadline and swiftly walked out of the room.

Redline was now worried.

"Oh, Barker, I didn't invite the security team to any of the stand-ups and left that security story in the backlog! It's not even in our sprint!" she confessed, becoming increasingly anxious.

They both realised that this meant they would now be behind regardless. Even if the DevOps team was ready to ship their product, they could not do so without receiving the blessing from the security team.

Barker turned bright red and admitted, *"I missed that too. We all missed it, and Maverick knows this. I will not stand for unnecessary governance and problems that cause us to miss our release date. I will tell the Security Manager to sign off on it or at least give us a waiver!"* he proclaimed.

Redline nodded firmly.

"Oh boy, the security team loves being told to 'just do it'," she muttered, sarcastically, to herself quietly.

Automaton gliding down the corridor and entered the room where Barker and Redline were.

"Sir, you wanted to speak with me?" he asked in his mechanical voice.

"Ah, yes, good timing." Barker paused, searching for the original reason he had summoned Automaton, his mind on something else entirely.

Redline was concerned with how Automaton and other team members were allocating their time. They were clearly not working in the agreed sprint plan.

Redline glared at Automaton.

"The stories that we didn't agree on and extra time on the Test Driven Development work that isn't expected for a least a few more sprints," Redline gritted, prodding Barker's memory, practically chiding him for forgetting.

"Oh, yes," recalled Barker. *"Redline and the team observed you working on items that were not part of the agreed upon sprint, and, I'm told you spent all last week automating a bunch of integration that isn't needed at this time."*

Automaton, although guilty of the charges, remained his matter of fact, robotic self. *"I kept busy with work that I felt needed to be done,"* he replied, flatly.

Redline did not want to blame the whole problem on Automaton. Seeing an opportunity for Automaton, who was very efficient, to help the team, she proposed, *"There are several tasks the team is working really hard on to close. Could you help them?"*

"Of course, Madam. It would be my pleasure," Automaton replied and glided off to find out who on the team was slow.

Redline, glad to avoid the potential creation of a blame culture, exhaled a sigh of relief.

Barker nodded. *"Yes! Thankfully, he agreed because I would have ordered him to do it otherwise!"* he declared before storming out of the room to figure out how to get his product released while dealing with the new security patch priority.

Redline watched him leave, chuckling to herself, *"Servant leader at his best."*

The points to address in effective communication hark back to those in Act I of *A Goal Driven Approach*.

It is crucial to understand that a goal driven approach is fundamental to Agile and DevOps evolving and adoption and transforming teams being constructive with effective processes, producing valuable products. Recognising this key point shall help Big Corp and Barker's DevOps plan mature the DevOps program into a DevOps-as-a-Service.

Figure 36 shows that they are in the storming phase. Many great things are happening, but turbulence is occurring because many things are new and potentially disruptive and chaotic, lacking refinement.

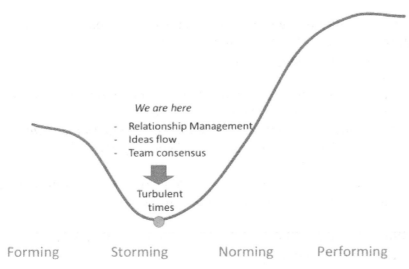

Figure 36 - Turbulent "Storming" times. Adapted from Tuckman's Stages of Group Development

The team realises and understands that paddling together is hard. Especially when waves, such as getting consensus, cause them to lose momentum and, potentially, perspective. Some folks like to be asked what to do where some like to be told.

Just as with paddling a boat, when we work together, we pull together, keeping what our teammates are doing in view to remain in sync. This takes practise and requires collaboration and leadership from within. Good stakeholder and relationship management, and openness to trying new things are another part of the equation.

Typically, a team moves from **forming** to **storming.** Teams can go south (badly), so this is a great time to experiment and learn. Remember fail-fast? Redline was doing the right thing by wanting to support her team while also remaining aware of what Automaton was saying, doing and feeling. Asking questions is a great starting place to uncover the rationale, motivation and behaviour a team member is displaying.

Boat Comes Ashore - The Retrospective

The first sprint was over, and it was time to review how it went in, what Agile processes call, a Retrospective.

The AoCs and all team members were present for the Retrospective. Barker chaired the meeting since he was the Product Owner and Redline was the scribe.

"Welcome to our first Retrospective," announced Barker. *"The AoCs have asked us to, first, make sure everyone understands the ground rules to help this be effective and valuable if and when critical concerns and conversations arise."* He uncovered a whiteboard with the guidelines listed.

1. Be directly honest
2. Be safe
3. Solve as a team
4. Share the solution with others

"Because this is our first Retrospective," Agent 77 began, stepping to the front of the room. *"I want to provide a few tips, so we contribute effectively, safely and collaboratively. If you are taking*

notes, you may also want to read some good points in the Opensource Article - Better Agile Retrospective Meetings – (Louis, 2018)," he advised.

Many of the team had heard of Retrospectives but found them to be boring and a waste of time.

Agent 77 uncovered another whiteboard, containing a list.

Retrospectives help identify:

1. *What is working*
2. *What is not working*
3. *Next steps to improve what we can improve*

"So, for DevOps teams, the art of proving a hypothesis - testing and sharing the success, then building on that to learn and improve your way of working - makes a team go from canoes to speed boats!" he exclaimed.

Barker gave him a thumbs up while turning to his team. *"What have we found challenging and not working for us?"* he inquired.

The room was silent, no one wanted to speak first.

Wiggles pointed at Automaton, complaining about him automating everything and slowing down the team. He returned fire, pointing at her with accusations of his own. Before long, a full-blown blame game had ensued, as the team pointed their fingers and argued.

"Perhaps, it is best to start with what is going well," Agent 9 remarked quietly to his colleagues. All the AoCs nodded.

Redline turned to Barker and let out a sigh. *"Well, at least the team is unified in their blaming!"*

Barker was horrified at the team's behaviour, frantically attempting to write down their complaints.

 Root Cause Analysis – Barker failed to ask the five WHYs during the Retrospective. The team only looked at WHATs, and some may have formulated their own idea around the HOWs.

The AoCs silently took notes and observed as the Retrospective continued. After the meeting finally adjourned, well over the intended end time, the AoCs excused themselves and, grabbing a snack and drink, headed back to the Dock.

"What the heck just happened?" Agent 13 spouted.

Agent 9, still wide eyed, took a bite out of his cookie.

Agent 77 stirred his tea and shook his head.

"Well, it's definitely storming! We have hit turbulent waters!" he joked, half-seriously. *"Look, we all knew that Barker, taking on the role of PO, was to be a learning process, bound to need extra guidance from us.*

"Now that the team has worked through a sprint together, there are many opportunities to improve. We are at a critical stage, and Maverick, Barker and the team, especially Barker, need guidance," he stated in a calm, confident tone.

It is important to consider how motivation affects behaviour and is related to the mindset. Discussed earlier, the concept of mindset and its link to hypothesis driven development is applicable to what happened in the Retrospective. Behaviour al Driven Development (BBD), now an extension of Test-Driven Development (TDD), facilitates collaboration between teams and individuals.

The AoCs dissected the events of the Retrospective, arguing that behaviour *was* the mindset. Agent 77 developed a partial behaviour model (Figure 37) to examine why this concept is so important.

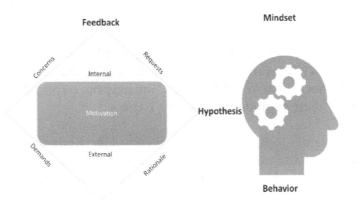

Figure 37 - Motivation Model - Behaviour

Notice that feedback is either internal or external, positive or negative, and can come from various angles such as:

- Concerns
- Demands
- Requests
- Rationale

Each of these areas form a feedback decision point in our brain, motivating us based on an idea or assumption, even if the data we believe is concrete (what we see, saw, or heard). The decision point affects our behaviour and the way we decide to act, which can be emotive or logical (or possibly a bit of both), with one side bearing a bit more weight, depending on the person, context and situation.

Feedback drives our motivation, which drives our behaviour, which becomes our mindset. Ideally, we want to have the best feedback possible coupled with the best mindset to make the best decisions. Of course, decisions need to be based on goals, shown earlier in Figure 6.

The AoCs needed to guide the team, and a useful exercise is to perform a **root cause analysis** on several issues that arose in the Retrospective. They suggested Rabbit, who was chairing the next Community of Practise, include this as a discussion topic since the CoP is a great place to share findings, perform analysis and provide feedback!

The outcome at the Retrospective was not what Barker expected and word got back to Maverick, who was not pleased. Barker had several things to resolve with another Team Lead (Scrum Master) on a different project, which was going off the rails.

He decided to focus first on the DevOps project by providing support on the roadblocks that Maverick and others had recently put in place, affecting them before the next sprint. The roadblocks were:

- Needing to provide a security patch before they could ship
- Finishing stories not completed to be ready to ship
- Automation tasks for the sprint stories ahead of the non-completed stories potentially affecting quality

Later that day, Redline decided to have a critical conversation with Barker. During the sprint, he realised that setting up meetings before he and Redline were aligned was not a good idea, so for the first time in many years, he opened his door to unplanned meetings and discussions. Formal meetings wasted time, and the highest priority of the Product Owner and Team Lead was resolving roadblocks.

After Redline and Barker rehashed the issues that came up in the Retrospective, specifically with Automaton, Barker asked Redline to find out what went wrong and why things started to derail when the team missed their agreed upon stories. He also asked her to come back later to review her findings along with a **burndown chart**.

Redline finished her meeting with Barker and texted Agent 9. She needed to consult any available AoCs.

Agent 9 waited for Redline at the Dock, greeting her as she approached.

"I remember the coaching class the AoCs led before the Retrospective where you guys spoke about root cause analysis and how to get to the root cause by asking why up to five times," she recalled, hoping he did too.

"Yes, we showed a diagram that looked something like this," he confirmed, pulling an illustration from a folder on his workspace (Figure 38). *"What about it?"*

Figure 38 - Root cause analysis

Redline reviewed the drawing in Agent 9's hand and nodded.

"That was it. I just needed to see the diagram again. Thank you!" she exclaimed, dashing off to uncover the root cause of why Automaton worked on other things rather than sticking to the stories and collaborating with the team.

Agent 9 smiled. *"Finally, an easy problem to solve!"* Agent 9 thought to himself as he tucked the diagram back into its folder pocket.

Weathering the "Storms at Sea"

The following day, Redline decided to apply root cause analysis when having a critical conversation with Automaton. She went over to his workspace and began asking why he made the decision to complete work items that were not in the current sprint backlog. Automaton did not offer much of a reason, so the conversation continued with Redline asking why but receiving no explanation until she had an "a-ha" moment, which came after Redline finally uncovered the rationale behind Automaton's rogue behaviour.

"So, what you're saying is that you decided to automate all of the tasks that you've been repeatedly doing during the stories in the current sprint. Specifically, you created automation scripts for when a developer modifies their code and deploys or updates a change to the repository, saving many minutes a day and lessening the chance of introducing bugs that are harder to fix later?" she recounted his explanation back for clarity.

Automaton click and whirred. *"Correct, Redline. Many of the tasks were taking too long to do manually and were all repetitive. Therefore, I created scripts to speed up the process and improve quality, which introduces a more test-driven development (TDD) approach to our coding and testing practises."*

"Oh," Redline blushed. She did not fully understand TDD or realise that Automaton's work reduced the number of mistakes, improved quality and increased the productivity of the development team.

Redline paused for a moment. *"Okay, I think I understand. Does this mean some of the stories and work items may require less effort? Does this change the size of the tasks in the next two sprints or reduce complexity?"*

Automaton replied, *"Yes. I also added the security patch validation routine in the automation script while completing your request to help other team members. Now, we can test the patch when we start the integration, regression and other tests!"*

Redline was impressed. *"You mean we already got the security patch in UAT (user acceptances test area), and you can just push a button to go to production?!?"*

The whirring stopped as Automaton spoke in a lower tone, *"Almost, my lady. We need to add the automation story to the next sprint and make sure the operations team is comfortable with automating these tasks. However, it will still take someone from Ops to accept the notification and permit the changes. In addition, we need to do some automation rolling back as it were if the previous state, so that the environment is exactly as it was if there are any issues with the deployment."*

Redline understood that this was a tall order, and working with Ops was a challenge at the best of times. Ops was so busy with black out dates, burning issues, change management requests, etc. It overwhelmed her just thinking about it all.

"To be frank, it is going to take a lot of work and major mindset changes for the Ops team to go along with this," Automaton confided.

Redline nodded, emphatically.

Automaton paused his blinking, *"All in appropriate time. Maybe we can convince them. It is not like we are automating everything..."* he quipped as he warped back to his station.

Redline and Automaton touched on a quite a few areas:
- Trust
- Integration
- Automation
- Improving the work process
- Team collaboration

Although Automaton understood TDD and saw the potential of using this process, he let the team down by not communicating and being transparent about what he was working on. Still, he was able to achieve many good things for the team, including "looking ahead" on both stories and tasks to see how they impacted the application and infrastructure.

Earlier in the project, Agent 77 spoke to the team about *"look ahead modeling"* and *"proving the architecture early,"* which Automaton was able to research and try, in practise, while they did their first sprint. However, while Automaton engaged with architecture and operations, he left out his DevOps project team members, such as the Product Owner, Barker, and his Team Lead, Redline. It is a good practise to keep them in the loop, especially when covering key milestones such as proving the architecture early.

Redline and Automaton were building trust in each other, making Automaton feel more secure to try things out...with the Product Owner's approval. He can now also go to Redline for help, approaching Barker.

Redline learned a lot about improving performance and quality by integrating the coding practises and automating much of the manual testing. She now understood this to be referred to as **continuous integration (CI)**.

The team then took it to the next level by adding automation to the security tests and many operational tasks to these CI processes. With this incorporated into their current sprint, they were able to implement the urgent patch, patching and deploying without having to start a new sprint. A CI mindset, using automation, helped operations get that patch out right away, as Maverick wanted, and connected it with their application while testing both at the same time in their systems environments. It was a success!

Automaton also improved his relationship with the operations team by demonstrating that his TDD process and work benefitted theirs as well! Being transparent and helping reduce operational risk was earning everyone's trust too.

Building a Better Boat – the "CoP"

When it comes to improving our way of working, which is a common goal across the DevOps lifecycle, many folks do not understand the fundamentals or how to measure success.

Businesses have questions, and the speed of business requires us to provide accurate, timely, qualitative and reliable feedback from our customers and stakeholders. Getting everyone on the adoption boat is not a trivial pursuit, it takes time and patience! Most importantly, many folks will not adopt something unless it demonstrates value, especially to their role and career. Transformation is a huge task, and with understanding, developing and implementing solutions iteratively comes learning and improving.

The CoP consists of **DevOps Practitioners**. Just like the guilds from days of old, practitioners need a place to share ideas, safely and effectively, to learn and grow. Unfortunately, many times, CoPs start with a bang then fizzle out.

When you start a community of practise, it is important to think about **terms of reference** (ToR) or a manifesto. This documents the purpose and mission of the CoP.

When creating your purpose, consider including these concepts:

- CoPs are made up of volunteers and people should be encouraged to join one if able to give and receive value.
- When and where the CoP is held matters.
- Choose topics and goals that spark interest and curiosity while also aligning to business, IT and enterprise goals then determine a process for discussing and exploring them.
- Establish if and how any decisions will be made or actions items assigned
- Define metrics for measuring performance, accountability and effectiveness, using application of outcomes and shared learnings.

CoPs are a fantastic and a fundamental way of getting teams to share **good practises**. The DevOps mindset, adopted by Maverick's IT team and coached by the AoCs, began small, at the individual level, eventually expanding to Barker's team. With a CoP, these teams can help spread the word, communicating the mindset and good DevOps practises across IT and the business.

Checkout the Creating a successful Community of Practise (CoP) event (AoC, 2020) checklist.

For additional information, outside of the important aspects highlighted in this book, read **Choose Your WoW** by Scott Ambler (Scott W. Ambler, Mark Lines, 2019). This can help guide teams, wanting to improve their way of working, which is a key and common goal in Disciplined Agile.

Barker was excited to update Maverick on how Automaton and Redline collaborated to deliver on his request. He went to Maverick's office to share the good news.

"Maverick, we were able to successfully test and deploy the security patch along with the first drop of our solution!" he proclaimed.

Maverick looked up from his desk, unaware Barker had entered. *"Really? That is fantastic! How were you able to get that into your sprint so quickly?"*

Barker had hoped he would ask. *"Automaton saved the day using 'look ahead modeling' with the architecture owner. He created an automation script that added the patch to the test-build process as part of the continuous integration story we did in our last iteration."*

Maverick was clearly happy. *"Excellent! We should share this with the operation and security teams to make sure they are agreeable to deploy as soon as possible!"*

"Agreed. I believe Redline and Automaton have already done so. My understanding is that operations will treat this as a special 'one-off' pilot to see if automating security patches in UAT and push a button deployment could be included in the regular deploy process," he explained.

Maverick was now really impressed, getting up to shake Barker's hand. *"Well done! Your team is doing better than I would have predicted, given some of the hiccups faced. Please continue to work with the AoCs. It is obvious that their guidance has been very useful."*

"Right-o, sir! Will do!" Barker saluted, smiling all the way back to his desk.

DevOps Mindset Value 4 Goal Reached

 We have reached our fourth goal – **striving to always innovate and improve** beyond repeatable processes and frameworks.

Innovation and improvement must be baked into your processes and encouraged within your teams. Everyone can impart, suggest and develop great ideas if a safe and constructive workplace is cultivated.

The innovation Automaton and Redline embraced came about, partially, by chance, yet their collaboration and teamwork made it successful. A bit of planning how to innovate and improve during iterations or sprints can really make the difference between success and failure.

How a DevOps team executes work is called a lifecycle. There are many different lifecycles to choose from, but the choice should be made collectively by the team. All DevOps lifecycles have several key milestones that do not, necessarily, work for every sprint or deliverable. Again, the team should decide which milestones in the process they wish to include and when.

When DevOps teams embrace Agile ways of working and include discipline, the concept of implementing and following goals is second nature. However, many Agile practises do not include the concept of a full "delivery lifecycle" or using clear goals.

When the AoCs talk to organisations wishing to implement DevOps, they often point to one of these delivery lifecycles.

1. **Agile** – follows traditional Agile processes and includes three phases; inception, construct and transition

2. **Continuous Agile**– similar to the Agile lifecycle but typically has shorter inception and transition phases and is used frequently when deploying many features on the same product, iteratively

3. **Lean Agile**– uses a phased approach without the typical Agile ceremonies or timed sprints. Instead, teams self-organise, meeting and demoing when needed. This lifecycle requires teams to be familiar with Agile and Lean processes and lends itself well with operations, as there are no cadences. Stories and work items are regularly reviewed with the product owner and prioritised daily, so teams can "pull" the next work item that is flagged as high priority as they finish a work item.

4. **Continuous Lean Agile**– Similar to Lean Agile, this lifecycle uses TDD and/or BDD processes and heavy automation throughout its entirety. It is not uncommon for teams who choose this lifecycle to deploy using continuous integration, continuous delivery and, potentially, continuous deployment. There are no sprints or cadences, but it does contain key milestones, goals and decisions - from **inception** through **transition** into production. Many consider a continuous lean agile lifecycle as the "holy grail" of lifecycles to move to for DevOps as giants such as Amazon,

Google, Microsoft and others pull work that form features in seconds, right into their production systems. This means that users can get value (sometimes break value) in seconds.

Most DevOps teams aspire to implement a continuous delivery lifecycle, so that they can concentrate on creating features that bring rather than the deployment of them.

While development teams can use Scrum methods such as the Agile Lifecycle or frameworks, operations tends to struggle with this approach. This is due to the cadences and prescriptive nature of many so-called Agile frameworks. Thus, whatever your DevOps team choses as their delivery lifecycle and Agile approach, they will benefit from moving towards Lean continuous delivery.

All Agile lifecycles typically begin with a concept and planning stage, taking the team all the way through deployment and delivery into the customer's hands.

 Improving your way of working should never be an afterthought!

The Dock

"*I like how we suggested ways to improve, and the team naturally started implementing them, despite some surprises!*" Agent 77 stated.

"*Personally, I like the vibrant discussions we have observed during the CoPs and in the team areas.*

"*I would love to see more visual cues, such as whiteboard sketches and diagrams, as well as the leadership attending and engaging more consistently. But today's environment is still a lot better than the ghost ship we encountered a few months ago,*" Agent 13 acknowledged.

"*I agree. We are making progress, but the key is keeping the organisation engaged from the top down. If we start to lose the attention from the executive management for this mindset change, we risk undoing all that we have done so far,*" reminded Agent 9.

Boat Inspection

Command & Control – Stakeholders Own Everything

At the end of the day, the AoCs walked through a new Agile Development Team area that had recently been set up. There, they overheard a Product Owner, using the dreaded "my way or the highway" attitude. He was shouting things, like:

- *"I want you to work on these, not those, tasks next!"*
- *"I want you to complete development by the 13th and deploy to pre-production by the 20th."*
- *"I bought you bleeding edge tools to give invaluable skills to the team! Use them!"*

- *"No, this is not up for discussion."*

The AoCs stood with their mouths agape, thinking that this new "Agile" team was in a dire predicament. They looked around the new team area, noticing the majority of members sitting at their desks, looking resigned and as if waiting to sneak out and go home. Two, ghost-like engineers stood at the coffee machine in the cold and sterile team area, staring at their delivery schedule in disbelief.

As the AoCs approached, one of them looked up and said, *"We never agreed to these insane commitments and release dates! We're in for some serious overtime again."*

Agent 9 located the Product Owners office, walled off from the rest of the workspace. Agent 9 knocked and introduced himself.

"Have you heard about the line of autonomy that both Maverick and Barker are using with their teams?" Agent 9 inquired, pausing to gauge how the Product Owner would react to the guided coaching.

When the Product Owner's attention remained focused on him, Agent 9 continued.

"I happened to notice your team's resigned silence as you discussed schedules, work items and stories. I am part of the AoCs, hired to help guide organisations through transitions of culture and process. If you are interested, we would be happy to review the value of Lean and Agile practises and guide your team to encourage feedback loops," Agent 9 suggested.

The Product Owner still did not react. He continued staring at Agent 9, seemingly contemplating this proposal. Eventually, he spoke.

"Actually, I would really like that. We are under a lot of pressure from management to deliver faster than ever, and because they know this is an Agile project, they expect even more to be delivered...even faster!" he admitted.

"I understand," assured Agent 9. *"We can help. We always recommend that everyone understand and honour the fine line of autonomy, empowering and trusting your team!"*

Act 5

VALUE – A Brighter Horizon

A Final Morning Chat

Several seasons and sprints passed as Maverick and his department continued investing in the DevOps adoption across the IT department. Things had certainly improved, but not all the wrinkles had been ironed out.

After several weeks away, helping another organisation, the Agents of Chaos entered the main lobby of Big Corp one morning for a status meeting. Almost immediately, they were joined by Knight, who was visibly stressed.

"I really appreciate your coaching over the last year, specifically with us engineers, ensuring transparency and accountability to the business," Knight began, leading up to the cause of his stress. "Unfortunately, though, some have returned to their old ways." He frowned with concern in his eyes. The AoCs waited, patiently, for him to compose himself and continue.

"For example, Automaton said that the DevOps mindset and using Lean or Agile tools is extra work and, at times, an unnecessary overhead. I do not understand because he was once a believer but now says he has no interest in 'Agile voodoo'," Knight confessed, hopelessly. "This attitude… it's not helping the team progress, innovate, improve or forward plan. Honestly, it is weighing us down." He looked to the AoCs for help.

They had heard this before, knowing all too well that once they moved on from Big Corp, some things and people may fall back to the way they had been. It was a natural occurrence when the daily and constant support of guided continuous improvement was removed.

"It will take time and effort to silence the critics. The secret solution includes transparency, collaboration, and continuous learning … with a pinch of tenacity and patience," Agent 13 assured.

Knight still looked concerned. "I know, but how can we ensure that we continue get buy-in from everyone on our team and across the organisation? How?" he pleaded.

"Let's go over to the Dock and look at the adoption roadmap, which still has several tactical pieces of work to discuss. We can also confirm that our strategic goals are not only valid but also still valuable," Agent 77 suggested.

Agent 9 patted Knight on the shoulder. Once at the Dock, they gathered around the roadmap.

"Let us identify and focus on the lowest hanging fruit. These work items ..." Agent 9 pointed to several unfinished tasks. *"...have been prioritised, and, these..."* He pointed to the burn-up charts. *"...illustrate which are key initiatives that Barker, our Product Owner, has already identified."*

Knight looked at the large touch screen as Agent 9 selected the Adoption Dashboard. Agent 9 then selected the current backlog as an example, zooming in on the burn-up charts to reveal which teams were experiencing challenges.

"We need to focus on the potentially least effective team, and they must be open for candid feedback. If we can guide them by addressing areas where there are challenges and review their Retrospectives, we would have an opportunity to help them become more effective," Agent 9 outlined.

"This kind of help inspires a team and possibly leads them to become a reference team, acting as both an example and catalyst for positive change to the rest of the organisation, motivating others to adopt and transform," he stated, hopefully.

Knight exhaled with relief. He regained some optimism and took a photo of the link for the dashboard to review with his colleagues back at his desk.

The AoCs followed Knight back to his area, noticing that the familiar maze of cubicles had been converted into open office spaces, buzzing with noise from discussions around screens, whiteboards and sticky notes. In fact, even some of the meeting rooms had been removed to allow more space for open and vibrant discussions between Product Owners, Scrum Masters and engineers.

The AoCs saw the evidence of their coaching displayed in the physical removal of barriers to promote transparency and collaboration but had concerns that it may have been taken too far.

"Wow, they really overreacted to our advice of creating an open environment to encourage transparency and collaboration. The noise, disruptions, and toxic context switching is distracting and having the opposite affect of its intention," Agent 13 remarked to his colleagues.

The AoCs all agreed this was not the open plan they recommended at all. Someone decided to just remove the cubicles and offices without thought to ambient noise, pods or other important working environment factors.

 Open office spaces can foster transparency, collaboration and face-to-face discussions. Unfortunately, they also promote distractions, noise, "opening themselves up to" excessive context switching and forcing users into drastic and detrimental habits, such as tuning out with noise-cancelling headsets, hiding in other parts of the office or working from home, as a way to focus on their commitments.

When you embrace an open office plan, take time to plan how the space will support effective teams. One should think of creating areas for teams to brainstorm at a whiteboard, host their daily scrum and planning and review ceremonies, or simply relax without distracting everyone else. Pods are great for grouping a small number of desks and technologies for team collaboration while quiet areas and desks are needed for individual work when focus or deep concentration is required.

Power Boats & Submarines

With more guidance, teams continued to reap the benefits of the lines of autonomy, and managers could see the value in self-organised teams. DevOps and Agility continued to be popular catch phrases and sought after project teams.

The tools and techniques discussed early in the DevOps adoption, such as continuous integration and bringing operations into automated deployments, resulted in business value being realised sooner than later. Automation became the norm, increasing the delivery of management's projects, often exceeding their expectations.

The changes in organisation, spaces and processes were very apparent, and the AoCs were glad to see adoption becoming widespread. Maverick decided to check in with the AoCs since they were now typically only on site once a week and their contract ended in less than a month.

"Have you seen the latest videos and promos for DevOps that we recently published on the IT home page?" Maverick asked proudly. *"We have made phenomenal progress, are still improving, and the Overlords could not be happier. In fact, our recent IT survey is showing its highest rated level of staff enthusiasm, interest and general happiness. You boys really changed the culture here and got us on the right track!"* Maverick

commended, walking over to the large touch screen and pressing the dashboard shortcut. He pointed to the latest burn-up charts and number of projects delivering features on a bi-weekly basis.

"Not only do the transparent updates enable all of us to familiarise ourselves with the overall system, they also highlight the Unicorn ... our digital transformation. We have empowered everyone to embrace an Agile and DevOps mindset organisation-wide!" lauded Maverick.

"Wow," Agent 13 said to Maverick. *"You are certainly full of vim and vigour today!"*

Maverick blushed.

"It is great that you and the rest of the organisation are realising the benefit of Agile and DevOps, recognizing the difference in both words as well. I think I can speak for all the AoCs *when I say that we are very pleased with the progress,"* Agent 13 congratulated an even redder Maverick.

Agent 77 stepped forward.

"Yes, it is great to see the enthusiasm and progress going in the right direction, however there is no end to continuous improvement. Victory is achieved with small wins as each goal in the organisation is realised and new, even better goals are planned, measured and met," he advised.

Just then, Barker poked his head into the Dock and greeted everyone.

"I could not help but overhear the last parts of your conversation, and I have to say, things are going rather swimmingly.

We have some great DevOps patterns we can use across IT and I believe---"

"Yes, you are right! Great patterns, widespread positivity, all of it!" Maverick cut him off to agree.

The AoCs were not used to this side of Maverick…or Barker.

"Even though it is far too early to ring the victory bells, I sense we are forgetting that the line of autonomy includes the team, choosing their way of working. We cannot force them to use a particular pattern just because it may work for another team," reminded Agent 13.

"Agreed, Agent 13. Choice is very important as is innovation and learning to improve our patterns that, of course, can but not must be shared with others," Agent 9 said, hoping to emphasise both sides of the coin as he expected both Maverick and Barker to be a bit annoyed. And he was right.

Maverick became visibly annoyed by the AoCs' cautions, speed bumps and reminders while Barker became annoyed at the AoCs simply for making Maverick annoyed!

Agent 77 politely tried to diffuse the tension.

"Gentlemen," he began. *"You and your teams have much to celebrate, and we want you to experience continued and sustainable success. We are concerned that a command-and-control approach may resurface if not careful. We fully support re-use and good patterns in behaviour, process and improved outcomes,"* he validated.

Maverick calmed down a bit.

"I suppose you are right," he said, letting out a chuckle. *"With all my excitement and thinking we have the making of a complete transformation and widespread adoption, I forgot that we do have a*

much longer journey ahead. There are still treacherous waters and sharks to watch for and avoid."

Barker nodded. *"This is very true and actually what I originally came down here to discuss with you. We certainly have many obstacles to navigate still, and I feel we could use your help in doing so. We need your help in the months ahead, I believe,"* professed Barker, hoping the AoCs had the bandwidth to continue supporting their transformation.

"This is precisely why we come by for DevOps and Agile tune-ups," smiled Agent 13.

"Exactly," echoed Agent 9. *"We want to help your teams excel beyond effective to truly exceptional, awesome and high-performance teams!"*

"Agents, thank you!" Both Maverick and Barker beamed with pride, optimism and gratitude.

Mass Producing the Crew & Boat

For the next few weeks, Barker took Maverick's instructions to heart. Maverick wanted high-performing teams, not just effective ones. Barker also wanted to replicate his team's success across IT and convince the other departments to join their Agile cause.

Barker, with the AoCs' help, created a training and education plan, ensuring he had certified training courses on Lean, as well as Agile, that could be scaled. Barker convinced the department heads to let their staff take the certification training and testing, which they went along with, because Maverick agreed to pay for it.

Training went on for several weeks, in multiple classes, both in person and virtually. Some of the department heads discussed what they learned and realised that, for agility at scale, they had to admit that delay and waste was a big reason for missing their goals and a bigger part of their performance issues.

Much of the Lean training focused on value, cost of delay and improving flow, so Barker and the department heads setup a task force to analyse business, development, and testing across value streams, using guidance from the AoCs, whiteboards and digital screens turned into detailed operational dashboards. During the development of value stream diagrams, the AoCs and task force identified the steps of how value was obtained from the customers' perspective.

The group also created value streams for internal stakeholders, looking for delays and handoffs as they did so. They used red ink to highlight a delay in value and waste. This exercise really illustrated that value was not being managed by the leaders, nor was the cost of delays.

The sharing and reuse of solutions to challenges and delays proved to Maverick that you cannot "clone" people. However, some processes, tools and ways of working can be adopted by more teams if it was fit for purpose rather than dictated.

The resulting speed improvement or velocity was significant, and many department heads bought into supporting Agile and using the teams with a DevOps mindset that Maverick and Barker had enabled.

 By focusing on the customer and removing waste, the business accelerated value-improving performance and stayed ahead of the competition. Business value is not just increased revenue and market share but also decreased risk and expense, built-in quality, and delighted users.

Disgruntled Passengers & Crew

As teams take responsibility and accountability for their features, they move from the **storming** to the **norming** stage (Tuckman, Bruce, 2019). When they reflect on their organisation as a complex and adaptive system, they begin to recognize that the features and products they develop belong to it. Thus, they see the enterprise as a whole as well as their contribution to the system. Teams also begin to see themselves as a reflection of that system as a whole, which is part of design thinking and a major shift from a single project to a product mentality, with enterprise awareness (as a principle) in mind.

Teams adopting this become resistant to the chaos created by known- and unknown- unknowns, resilient to churn, and champions of change for other, less-Agile and new-to-DevOps teams.

As they learn and collaborate, sustainably, and performance improves, they begin the transformation to the realm of high-performing teams who are competent, autonomous, self-organising, cross-functional, and capable of handling complex issues and decentralised decision-making. They are trusted by the business and a major force for change that brings value with predictable velocity. These high-performing teams evolve into a group of stakeholders that are highly motivated, strategically aware, and goal and data driven, capable of dealing with most challenges the ocean presents them.

Maverick understood this to some extent, however he was motivated by other factors, including his impending retirement and desire for fast results at almost any cost. He valued his staff and leaders, yet still sought out a long-lasting legacy he could leave behind soon.

Maverick arrived at his weekly catch-up with the AoCs with his 'unicorn legacy' still on his mind.

"Good morning," the AoCs greeted. Maverick's smiled faded as he looked over at one of the large touch screens and saw new metrics

and scoring data flashing on a dashboard. He pointed at the monitor, *"What was that? Bring that back up!"* he said, rather angrily, to the AoCs.

They had received these results the day before and spent hours deciding how to present them to Maverick and Barker.

Agent 13 recalled the results to himself, *"The ambitious plans to scale the entire organisation are starting to show cracks. Satisfaction scores, quality, and morale is on the decline."*

Agent 9 projected the 'Organisation to Project - Performance and Goals' dashboard onto the screen, displaying the results.

"We were discussing this yesterday and analysing data, based on past feedback and trend analysis, to better understand what is happening here," Agent 77 consoled.

Maverick knew the AoCs were usually on top of things, so he did not panic. He spoke in a low and concerned voice, *"I'm confused. I have seen the data and many teams are displaying perfect burn-down charts, overall deployment frequency is increasing, and lead-time for change is decreasing. Everyone is working extremely hard! I don't get it..."*

"It would be a good idea to hold a Retrospective on this tomorrow, and a "what and why" meeting with our Product Owners and Scrum Masters beforehand, bringing everyone in later to validate the findings for a how, when and where," Agent 9 extended.

"Great idea", Maverick exclaimed, *"My unicorn legacy is going up in smoke, and I want to stop the fires asap!"* He checked his phone for his availability. *"Tomorrow, 9am sharp, I will cancel my other meeting as this is high priority."* They all plugged the meeting time into their calendars then Maverick went on his way, mumbling about unicorns, fires, and high priorities.

The AoCs were intrigued by the results of the most recent surveys and somewhat so by the unicorn legacy Maverick mentioned. They continued gathering as much information as they could to better understand the root cause or underlying problems, wanting to cite real data in the meeting, not conjecture.

They worked late into the evening, taking only a short coffee and snack break where they revisited Maverick's meaning behind his unicorn legacy. Agents 77 and 9 laughed, *"I guess he wants to leave a real mark of success when he retires in the next year or two…"*

Agent 13, however, did not find it amusing.

"Guys, we have a real problem here; Maverick is putting his own self-interest ahead of his team and colleagues. I really dislike that," he scolded.

The others laughed it off, reminding him that some leaders' self-interests can still be motivators to help drive the right success. They must continue to utilize the power of the wave Maverick had started. Without him, none of them would have had the chance to make any difference at all!

Storm Chasers for Brighter Skies

Later that week, a workshop to examine root cause issues and findings around the performance, scaling and other factors was held at the Dock. A large table was added in front of the whiteboards in the AoCs' area, holding large touch screen TVs and monitors. The AoCs brought plenty of snacks from the canteen (cafeteria) to lighten the mood and engage the brains.

After Maverick and Barker opened with some of the concerns they had, the baton was handed to the AoCs to guide and facilitate the remainder of the workshop.

Agent 13 scribbled the familiar forming-storming-norming-performing diagram on the whiteboard with an arrow, pointing to the area in between norming and performing.

"This is where we should be by now," Agent 13 stated. *"However, many of the teams that were norming and headed towards performing have regressed. In fact, some have either failed to move ahead, never leaving the storming stage or, worse, run out of steam, reverting back to storming."*

Agent 13 added two dashed lines to the diagram, pointing to storming and morning, as shown in Figure 39.

Figure 39 – Performing, or not? Adapted from Tuckman's Stages of Group Development

Agent 13 paused to allow the AoCs to observe the reactions from the group. Interestingly, no one objected or blamed one another, which was a positive sign of progress.

Agent 13 then continued, gesturing on the touch screen and displaying the DevOps adoption roadmap.

"Looking at this dashboard and some of the overlaid velocity metrics, we can clearly see that training the entire organisation was an invaluable exercise. However, notice the adoption roadmap included education specific to leaders, business and IT teams.

"Unfortunately, a decision was made not to tailor the courseware for these audiences but rather to use the out-of-the-box certification training guided by external instructors or online courses. Per the training feedback forms, experienced teams became frustrated by

this as they expected specific, more advanced and relevant instruction."

Barker and Maverick took notes, knowing they had made and agreed to this decision. This explained why performance was suffering. Agent 77 stood up and opened a new window on the touchscreen that displayed a graphic of teams, their utilization and associated projects.

"Starting about a month ago, the data shows a common pattern of distributing resources across teams. For example, Barker, your teams were performing really well. Yet , the decision to break up Redline's team and distribute the members across other teams resulted in a decrease in velocity, which directly impacted performance.

"In fact, the very next sprint shows testing was delayed in the former team, which caused quality issues in both. When a high-performing team is dismantled, we run the risk of losing cohesion and harmony. Not only did Redline's high-performing team suffer, the other teams were also impacted by the new members, which was a major contributing factor to disruption and lost velocity," Agent 77 informed.

Barker knew it was a safe room. The AoCs had explained the importance of critical observations and conversations.

Agent 13 asked Umpty, *"We heard feedback from the Retrospectives that some team members reprimand other team members."*

Umpty looked even more uncomfortable than normal, his nerves on high alert. He nodded.

Agent 13 continued, *"It is understandable for us to feel stressed, especially when we are going faster than before, and the team is demanding more from everyone."*

Umpty relaxed slightly and replied, *"This is true. My team was doing several swarming, code katas and mob programming to collaborate on improving the continuous delivery pipelines. I kept telling them to return to their desks and write code as we had no time to concern ourselves with automation. I guess some of the team members got angry because they left the team."*

"Interesting," noted Agent 13. *"So, that must be one of the reasons we also saw a shift in team members in the middle of a sprint. Can we all see that the resultant toxic atmosphere eroded trust, autonomy, and purpose. This was counter-intuitive."*

"A very valuable lesson," Maverick said, looking at Umpty and Barker.

Agent 9 smiled at Umpty. *"It takes courage to share even when we may not want to, and it's very important for us to find out what is working or not working. Well done, Umpty!"* he commented, walking up to the touch screen.

"I also want to share some important findings we began seeing some time ago," he announced. *"We wanted to make sure our findings were correct, so we worked quite late the other night to pull data across the projects."* He displayed the information on the screen.

"Notice that, for many projects, teams are rated and ranked on their burndown charts. While we discussed using burndown charts as one of the options to measure how teams are doing, it was not the best tool for the job in the end. Looking at these, we can see some teams overcooked the time they needed by increasing their story points for tasks that, in the past, took them much less time. There were some other kinds of cheats used as well.

"Gaming the system only makes this a vanity metric, which encourages gamification over innovation. In fact, we can see Redline's team, who used burn-up charts and other measuring tools, stabilized much quicker and saw improved performance. The lesson here is that if we create self-serving tasks, closing them like clockwork, teams are grooming their burn down charts instead of delivering business value, reducing risk, and increasing quality," Agent 9 explained.

Everyone understood clearly now, seeing the validity of choosing how they work with thought, not just going through the motions.

"We see this with many teams," Agent 13 chuckled, reassuring the group. *"Believe me, this happens, which is why we are reviewing, discussing and learning. I would also like to add to Agent 9's observation by showing you a few delivery pipelines with disabled automated tests and several without evidence of any unit, integration, or other test strategies."* He pulled up the examples on the screen. *"Although the deployment frequency is up, it is garbage in, which means garbage out!"*

This was many key points, and the AoCs sensed it was time to call a break. Redline and the other Team Leads gave silent acknowledgement and appreciation nods to the AoCs, thankful to finally have their concerns expressed and actually heard. They had been in Barker's office letting off steam on a near daily basis, however, their feedback and recommendations had fallen on deaf ears.

"Wow, this is a lot to process," Maverick said, standing up to stretch his legs. *"After our break, let's discuss how to go from the root cause to suggested solutions."*

Barker pulled the AoCs aside, telling them that he had sensed and even heard some of these concerns from his teams before, but had assumed things would work themselves out. Rather than make excuses, Barker, who rarely apologises for anything, apologised to the AoCs. They advised him to do the same to his teams, which would encourage transparency and continued critical feedback.

Course Corrections

Do Not Fragment Your Teams

 Your stakeholders are invaluable knowledge workers. Think of them as **assets**, not simply as resources. Lead, guide and encourage them, rather than command and deploy them around, like ships scattered at sea!

"If everyone is moving forward together, then success takes care of itself." – Henry Ford (Ford, 2014)

The AoCs had compiled the feedback and root causes under three key areas.
- Stalling or not progressing from forming to norming
- Regressing or moving back from performing to norming
- Tiring out or not sustainably producing the peak performance they once so cherished

Next to each of the root causes the AoCs included some potential solutions, options and suggestions they had already discussed. What the team had not really realised was this was a "teams of teams" approach to following up on past Retrospectives. Each of the areas was up on a whiteboard, and everyone was given sticky notes and markers. They were asked to provide any other feedback and a suggestion they had proposed recently or in the past.

After about thirty minutes, the AoCs went over the results with the group. At this point, there were many others watching from the IT floor. They all seemed to want to know what items Maverick and Barker would deem as important priorities for the teams.

Everyone, with stickies and key areas in front of them, was asked to prioritise which they thought were the most important, Barker included. Although Maverick had the final say, being the key stakeholder and sponsor, it was important to collect feedback from everyone involved.

Barker, as the Product Owner (Director), began to understand what and why was needed to correct the courses of each of the project. He would now have to take the *what* and *why* to each project team and work with them to find out the *how*, *when* and *where* to determine getting to the solution. These were to become new work items included in their next sprints, encouraging them to monitor success or failure of applying each resolution.

The AoCs reiterated the definition of DevOps, including the point around Donovan's definition, which included "*union of people and process and products*".

"How do the teams put this into practise?" Barker asked the Agents.

"Ah," said the AoCs, collectively. *"Remember during our discussion on effective Retrospective, we talked about improving our WoW?"*

"That was the Plan, Do, Study, Act aspect that you guys talked about, right?" Barker hesitantly confirmed.

Agent 77 flipped a screen and showed the diagram, PDSA and the five steps to improving your WoW, using what PMI Disciplined Agile calls Guided Continuous Improvement, which extends the Kaizen loop - (PMI Disciplined Agile, 2020). He then showed the following picture which highlights this point.

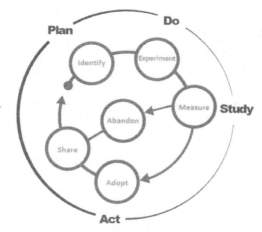

Plan: **Identify a potential improvement**
The team identifies a technique, either practice or strategy, that they believe works for them.

Do: **Try out the new WoW**

The team needs to give the experiment sufficient time to determine how well it works in practice.

Study: **Measure the effectiveness**

After you've run the experiment, you should assess how well it worked for you.

Act: **Adopt or abandon the new WoW**

Our advice is to adopt what works well for you and to abandon or better yet improve upon what doesn't.

Share learnings with others

When a team learns something about a technique, the implication is that they should share it with others.

Figure 40 – Agent 77's GCI using PDSA

Maverick said, *"I remember we planned to setup some training and coaching on this subject before your contracts are up. Let's discuss how you can help Barker and the teams put this into practise and get us back on track."*

"What do we do in the meantime?" asked Barker, expressing the group's collective concern.

"Not to worry, everyone," Agent 9 assured. *"You will find your secret sauce, that works best for each team. We have enough time to test this out with one of your teams before we go too.*

"However, the real secret sauce comes from teams interactively, safely and openly collaborating. The magic combination of compassion, integrity, trust, respect, experience, knowledge, skills,

and many other qualities builds a harmonious team. Continually improving on this will help evolve teams from norming to performing, resulting in them becoming highly effective." Agent 9 smiled at the group, hoping to spread his knowledge and optimism.

Agent 77 took a deep breath. *"The very cool and magical thing here, as Agent 9 aptly described, is that everyone's skills get better. In fact, many learn new ways of working growing their WoW. Team members become a T- or E-shaped crew that can adapt, self-organise and handle many different roles with their many different skills."* Agent 77 paused, sensing mild confusion in the crowd.

"The reason we call them T- or E- shaped is because they have several skills at different levels and one or more core skills they are really adept with. Thus, if we drew their skills in a model, it might look like the letter T or E," he clarified, successfully.

Agent 13 took over. *"Special Forces is an example of highly effective team members that are T-shaped in terms of experience and skills, based on integrity and trust, and typically remain with and operate as one team."* He held up one of the books he carried with him all the time. *"Another example is the USS Santa Fe submarine team, as documented in this book,* **Turn the Ship Around** *–* (Marquet, 2012). *"*

 Sunset projects, not teams! You cannot duplicate an effective team by distributing its members to other teams or continuously re-building teams around projects. Let them build, maintain and improve their own WoW, collectively and individually. When you make changes or force teams to do so, you are damaging their way of working and reducing, even potentially destroying, their effectiveness.

The AoCs continued to describe that the leaders, Product Owners and Scrum Masters / Team Leads need to support an exciting and empowering vision, combined with autonomy and purpose. This is key to pointing all teams and stakeholders in a common direction.

High-performing teams are energised by transparency, collaboration, and continuous learning, however, they are also sustainable and cared for, so they do not wear out. Please, please, do not replicate your organisational silos by creating special teams with boundaries and access restrictions to knowledge and resources. Instead, encourage teams to have an insight into your strategic portfolio and share each others' backlogs, repositories, and pipelines.

"Maverick," Agent 13 continued. *"We are not saying that you should promote a common engineering system that reflects the Wild West, but one that creates a balance of team autonomy and organisational alignment around your core values, as shown in Figure 3."*

 "Good point. We may have been overzealous with our quest for fine-tuned engineering teams, working behind closed doors and our strict policy of least privilege," Barker admitted.

"Teamwork begins by building trust. And the only way to do that is to overcome our need for invulnerability." – Patrick Lencioni

It is important not to produce designs of your solutions or common engineering group setup, which are copies of your communication structures, as defined by Conoway's Law - (Mel Conway, 2019). Instead, follow the **Inverse Conway Maneuver** and encourage your organisation to promote an intentional and emergent design. For Azure DevOps (Microsoft, Visual Studio, 2019) users, that encourages the "one team project to rule them all!"

"While many leaders admire the Googles, Amazons and Microsofts of the world for producing and deploying code or features in seconds," Agent 77 then said with finality. *"This should not be your motivator or something you want to shadow. Each business is a complex adaptive system (CAS) made up of people, processes, products that are unique to your organisation, so you want to avoid*

*continuous shadowing. Your WoW is **your** WoW and, while we can admire others and even look at some of their WoW as potential solutions we may want to adopt, we are not these organisations and our vision is much different than any of them."* Agent 13, looking at the expressions of the group, was hopeful he had made his point clear.

Use blueprints and case studies as guidance, but do not attempt to replicate another high-performing organisation. Each has core values, vision, people, process and products that are unique!

Actionable Feedback & Validated Learning

The workshop continued for a while, covering many informative topics for improvement. The time was fast approaching to end these discussions and take the feedback and validated learning from the day's session to Barker for assistance understanding the *Plan, Do, Study, Act* concept in practise.

Everyone thanked the AoCs for a great session, who thanked them, in return, for contributing and being honest. As the clock struck 12:00pm, everyone headed to lunch except for Barker and the AoCs.

Together, they created a backlog of work items to plan the next session with the team of Barker's choosing.

Rabbit, always thoughtful, brought sandwiches and goodies to the Dock for a working lunch. The AoCs wanted to get things back on track and only had a few days before they were heading to their next gig. The group focused hard, working with Barker to improve one of his project's WoW and guide it into a continuous improvement process using Plan, Do, Study and Act.

Barker chose to work on a key issue around performance, so the AoCs reviewed burndown charts, which were not their preferred way of measuring team performance, but it was Barker's choice.

Agent 9 asked, *"You mentioned that teams are rated and ranked on their burndown charts and based on planned and completed tasks?"*

"Correct, we want teams to commit and deliver work, to ensure we can deliver business value in a predictable way. We also want to reward the teams that deliver as planned, without any distractions," Barker answered.

The AoCs continued stressing the significance of using proper metrics from the start. Barker explained that he and Maverick decided to exclude metrics from the pilot project in light of many teams losing interest with anything beyond burndown charts.

The AoCs understood but reminded him not to look for blame in the results or create doubt in the importance of relentless monitoring and feedback. They unpacked the need for actionable feedback and validated learning.

"Recall the Lean principle of taking an idea, building a minimally viable product (MVP) to baseline and testing assumptions and hypothesis, based on objective and measurable data we collect where it matters the most ... with the end-user, in production," Agent 77 proposed.

How data or evidence is gathered is not important. We can use a combination of market research, production telemetry, surveys, unsolicited feedback, customer visits, or the Gemba walk (Wikipedia, 2019).

We need to measure **everything** that is measurable and continuously gather, analyze, learn-from, and improve the telemetry, considering data as the validation to make smarter decisions. Similarly to the DevOps transformation, gathering empirical feedback is a continuous journey of innovation without a destination.

Measure everything that is measurable!

The art of fine-tuning what and how you measure data without inundating everyone with reports and notifications is an art and a necessity for a healthy DevOps mindset.

Product owners need fast feedback on feature ideas. Engineering needs continuous, full-stack telemetry on the quality of their code, non-functional requirements, and implementation of feature ideas. Your practise lead (domain expert) and guardian of manifestos, patterns, practises, guidelines, and governance need constant feedback from engineering.

Operations requires continuous and real-time telemetry to understand the health of the continuous delivery pipeline. Ops thrives on feedback, such as delivery lead time, deployment frequency, mean time to restore or recovery (MTTR), and failure rate. See Figure 12 for details.

Agent 9 then spoke, *"Before we park this topic and move on, I would like us to return to the burndown charts. Can you repeat what you told me earlier today at our break, Agent 13?"*

"Sure!" he exclaimed. *"I believe I said that when teams are measured on their burndown charts and punished for changing the planned tasks for the iteration or sprint, encouraging a rigid and intentional design. The resulting mindset will be to design what needs to be done, execute on what was designed, reprimand developers who deviate (innovate) from the plan, then deliver what was built ... fingers crossed. Sounds like a mini-waterfall within an iteration, to me."*

Agent 77 looked over at Barker, agreeing, *"Sounds too much like a process that is ripe for gaming!"*

Barker was confused. He did not know what the AoCs were referring to. *"Gaming? I do not know about that! We focus on a set of deliverables and make sure that we deliver value after every iteration. My team, for example, has perfected their iteration lifecycle and usually wins the burndown challenge.*"

Agent 13 shook his head, "*Are you sure that is exactly what is going on? From my vantage point, your team has merely perfected the art of breaking stories down into tasks, which they close with the help of their Scrum Master while continuously watching the burndown trending line, often keeping completed tasks open or postponing opening tasks they are working on. This is gamification, not value delivery.*"

Barker, suddenly realising that his team was, in fact, gaming the system, was not going to tolerate it!

 Focus on valuable and empirical feedback. Feedback needs to be **deliberated** in your community of practise, transparently **shared** through formal training sessions and informal lunch & learns, and **validated** with relentless improvements tools like code katas, CoPs and hackathons.

Do not fall into the trap of vanity metrics and gamification, which will impact the value of and trust in feedback.

"*Remember, only a delighted user confirms the value of your deliverables. You must adopt an emergent design, in which you plan, do, study, and act (PDSA), which I refer to as the Kaizen Model. Your Agile development teams should not be measured on how well they manage their burndown charts, but on how they react to changing business requirements and technology, and (most importantly) user feedback. Aim for continuous feedback throughout the whole process, not just in response to an iteration or sprint deliverable,*" Agent 77 imparted.

 The goal is **delighted**, not just satisfied, users and stakeholders. This means both actionable telemetries are needed for engineering and user feedback for program management.

Barker was beginning to grasp the Kaizen Model using Plan, Do, Study Act. He was excited to move onto **what** data to collect, **why** it is important, **how** to share it and **how** to motivate, not measure,' teams.

You Need Built-in Quality!

Maverick was able to meet with the AoCs the next day. He was big on making governance work now that he could see Barker was correct. Good governance was an enabler to making his vision and legacy stand. They gathered in his office to discuss quality and governance from a Lean perspective as it complements the DevOps mindset.

The AoCs explained that an organisation's manifestos, Lean governance and standards must be reflected throughout and beyond the delivery lifecycle while including a product or feature's lifecycle and perspective. The lifecycle should go from idea and concept to deprecation and termination. **Quality** cannot be an afterthought or sprinkled across a solution, it is one of the most important aspects to the success of your product's ability to retain and grow customers.

Quality is an essential Lean pillar. It is not good to rely on unverified or unvalidated features. Where there is poor quality, there is waste. Waste is expensive and when we gamble with quality, we end up with expensive loopbacks from diligent testers and undelighted users, resulting in excessive and expensive rework and loss of satisfaction, trust and, ultimately, customers.

The AoCs had hard data showing feedback from the engineering teams, complaining about pull requests that promote pair reviews, continued learnings, and validated code, security, and system quality.

Maverick, remembering a conversation with Barker regarding long pull requests impacting performance, said, *"I have been told that pull requests now take up something like 10 minutes to validate,*

---

compared to the typical 1-2 minutes, and the teams are not hitting their story points. We are being slowed down by these infernal, long pipelines and the extra work from moving to DevOps that we did not expect."

Agent 13 knew where this was going and walked to the whiteboard and re-drew the pull request flow diagram for, what felt like, the 100th time (Figure 41).

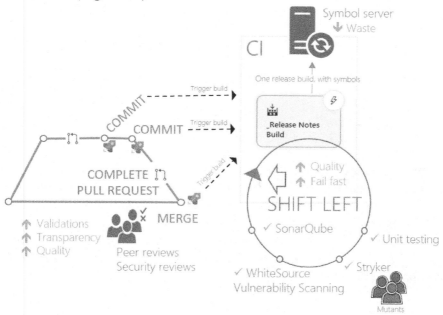

Figure 41 - Pull Request Flow

"OK, let us assume that everyone has finally agreed that feature branches are short-lived, and engineers will work on small and loosely coupled features. When finished, they promote their DRAFT pull requests to trigger a validation of the agreed policies and notify all designated reviewers.

"Let us further assume that it takes a few seconds for the notifications to be sent and emails to be actioned, and then, most importantly, a while for the reviewers to pair-review the pull request. In the meantime, engineers can take a well-deserved break or create another feature branch and start work on the next feature (

Figure 42). It does not matter if the validation build takes 10 minutes in parallel to review notifications being sent and processed."

"I agree," affirmed Agent 77. *"The point is not fast pipelines or expectations for a pull request to be approved within seconds. When the focus is on pure automation of fast pipelines, these become vanity reviews, unverified and unvalidated code changes, and risks of opening up the product to a lack of built-in quality."*

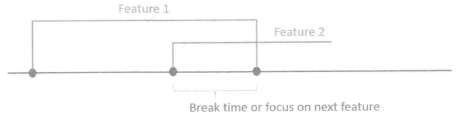

Figure 42 - Churn time — break or re-focus

Agent 13 continued, *"By investing in small, autonomous, loosely coupled, in-memory unit and integration tests you can create a deck of validations that can be run with EVERY pull request validation build or merge triggered continuous integration build. Take a minute to absorb Figure 43! It is not a mock-up. Rather, it is a snippet from a real delivery pipeline that the likes of Donovan Brown and I have presented with pride."*

Maverick had not expected to have this conversation and was in over his head. He really needed Barker and the developers to discuss this instead. He thanked the AoCs, informing them of this.

They agreed with him, stating that the fact that he supports it is crucial and that they had already scheduled time to meet with Barker and his team.

They found Barker and Redline together, discussing improving team morale and performance, and reviewed the pipeline discussion they had just finished with Maverick.

Barker expressed concern over how long the pipelines took.

Agent 13 frowned, *"Barker, what you should have noticed is that we are running 71,283-unit tests, or 180-unit tests per second, with a 100% pass rate. If the duration is a concern, configure your pipeline to run only unit tests that are affected by your code change. If you are making a revision to your aircraft, would you want to 71,000 validation tests or a fraction of that to ensure you can takeoff for your next (and potentially last) test flight?"*

Redline had been having this argument with Automaton on a regular basis. She said, *"When you put it into perspective that way, investing 6-7 minutes of our development time to take a mental break and grab a coffee while knowing our code change is scrutinised is worth every second!"*

Barker agreed and said, *"You're right, we can bake quality into our pipelines, working with the developers to understand the process and take advantage of pair programming, improved security and quality tests."*

Barker knew this was going to be a big challenge, however, working collaboratively and transparently with them so they understood the value of quality while the team builds the *how* would give them a sense of ownership, making it work for them while improving quality!

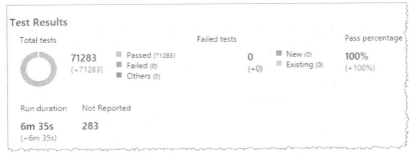

Figure 43 - 70000 Unit Tests is not a fallacy!

Do Not Tolerate GIGO!

Imagine going on your journey, having filled the engine with fuel, containing water or other impurities. Your trip would not last long...you would be stranded at sea! When you permit software written by inexperienced engineers, using the wrong tools and misaligned processes or a lack of standards, it allows impurities, poor quality and bad performance to occur, and this is not high quality.

Stop, do not encourage or support **Garbage In**, or you will inevitably get **Garbage Out**!

Garbage Stinks!

Do not try to obfuscate low-quality, untested, or unfactored code. You cannot mask the stench of garbage with an air freshener for long. Similarly, you cannot hide the absence or disregard of built-in quality in your people, process, or products. When (not if) the lack of quality surfaces, your users will lose all trust in you and your product and then the game is over for everyone!

Eradicate Technical Debt & Build in Innovation

"Agents, the architecture team is worried about technical debt. They have brought this up in a number of feedback sessions. Many of them feel that it is preventing innovation and improvements, which is also impacting quality," Maverick informed.

Barker saw the AoCs and Redline look to him, so he said, *"I asked all teams to keep track of the bugs, incidents, and technical debt, so that we can plan for and prioritise remediation."*

"Yes, remediation or refactoring, along with many qualities (performance, security, reliability) and modernizing your code will be impacted by unmanaged technical debt. The key here is to avoid or manage that by planning on how to pay that debt down," Agent 77 added.

Agent 9 showed examples of work items that addressed technical debt on his tablet. In other cases, he showed acceptance criteria that included reducing technical debt where the story would meet good practises and delight the user. *"I hope you're tracking and treating them differently,"* he remarked.

Maverick pondered for a moment, commenting, *"Well, we kind of are. We are also treating these technical debt pieces of work as bugs."*

"This could open up a can of worms," Agent 13 asserted after giving it some thought. *"In the context of software, a bug is a problem caused by low-quality code or erroneous logic, which results in a deviation from expected functionality. Always triage, prioritise, and remediate bugs, deploying fixes in forthcoming releases continuously.*

"The infamous 2AM call is a typical source of live site incidents and is often tied to non-functional requirements, such as performance, security, usability, or reliability. Immediately analyse and remediate

an incident, ensuring that you pivot the "hair-on-fire" user to a delighted user in production.

"Technical debt appears when you embrace workarounds or take shortcuts in your design, code, and architecture. Like skipping payments on your mortgage, technical debt accumulates and can stifle your team. Avoid technical debt or address it as soon as possible."

Agent 9 added, *"In other words, plan to remediate bugs as soon as possible and avoid, not plan, technical debt."*

Agent 77 was looking over the feedback from the architecture teams and noticed none of them was working with the DevOps team.

"Is anyone in your team taking on the role of Architect Owner? This is very important, even if your team member is a developer or operations guru, they need to make sure architecture communication is happening between teams! That way you can scale them to support big picture, Lean governance, standards and such across your teams."

Redline added, *"Thus, by including the Architecture Owner role as a member of the team and utilizing the suggested pull-request flows, we can address both technical debt and improve quality! I can now see that shifting our unit and integration testing as far left as possible will enable the reduction of bugs and incidents."*

"Excellent suggestions and very useful tactical and strategic solutions," Barker exclaimed. *"We can get our bugs and technical debt categorised and under control. Great progress to improve our built-in quality. AoCs, why and how is innovation really important though?"*

The AoCs stared at each other in disbelief. Agent 13 handed him a magnet for whiteboards that he had printed recently, stating:

- *Continuously learn*

- *Continuously refactor*
- *Continuously KAIZEN (Improve)*
- *Continuously transfer information*
- *Continuously INVEST SMART*

"Maybe this is a good time to take a break," remarked Agent 77 to an agreeable group. *"This isn't a small topic, and I could use one."*

Continuous and relentless learning, experimentation, improvement, and reflection allows us to continuously innovate and enhance, not just parts but the whole of our common engineering system, scaling later to include the entire organisation. As we are concerned primarily with DevOps engineering, the magnet highlights the mindset that enables engineers and business to continuously deliver value to delight users.

When teams create stories and work items in backlogs, it helps the business create great stories that facilitate Business and IT collaboratively, by using INVEST, enhancing the requirements to be Independent, Negotiable, Variable, Estimable, Small, and Testable. This also improves how teams validate assumptions and break down requirements into SMART stories that are Specific, Measurable, Achievable, Realistic, and Time-boxed.

By allowing engineering to use processes and products to automate manual and error-prone tasks to build, validate, and deliver quality features quicker, every time, all the time, the results lead to success.

Lastly, continuous innovation encourages relentless refactoring to improve readability, testability, maintainability, security, and quality of the binary DNA of the solution.

Observe how your kids install, evaluate, and replace applications on their mobile phones.

Zero tolerance for shoddy quality, zero loyalty to brands, and zero patience for imperfections. If an application does not work first time, it is uninstalled and replaced with another.

To delight the new generation of users, we need to continuously innovate, evaluate, pivot, and respond to an industry that is aggressive, relentless, competitive, and continuously changing.

Automate What is Automatable & Integrate

The next day, Barker and Redline requested a meeting with the AoCs at the Dock. The AoCs, on their last day at Big Corp, figured out the next move.

Barker was concerned that the team may be too focused on automation, neglecting other aspects of the project and doing too much for too little gain.

Redline described a constant tug-of-war with Automaton, pushing the "everything must be automated" line, which was conflicting with Knight and the rest of the team.

"AoCs, I am all for automation and support much of what Automaton is doing in the Pipeline for CI and CD, however, we are now working off a software as a service platform (SaaS), and this vendor handles a lot of the testing once the solution is configured, as it is a low-code option. I fear Automaton's quest for automation nirvana is making a lot of engineers spend time researching or developing solutions for the platform itself rather than the project," Redline confessed.

The AoCs understood this problem all to well and explained that a balance must be reached. Automation to a process should be considered when:

- The process is often repeated and has potential to speed up
- Quality can be improved
- Test first and Test Driven development is part of the plan
- Reduction in costs can be realised

"Yes, we had a chat with Knight a little while ago," recalled Agent 13. *"Automaton seems to be obsessed with automation, automating everything and giving everyone on the team a hard time for not embracing, what he calls, the core principle of DevOps."* Agent 13 waited for confirmation.

They all then discussed how they have each had numerous chats with Automaton to emphasise that DevOps benefits from, but it is not one in the same as, automation. He was passionate about automation, but unfortunately, overzealous to automate everything, even if it meant disrupting his relationships with his team members.

Agent 13 went on to describe some additional considerations for automating what is automatable.

"Manual tasks and processes are a smell on your DevOps journey and a toxin for continuous delivery, consistency, efficiency, auditability, and maintainability. You may also hear that manual processes nurture complexity; however, automation can be over engineered and complex as well. Whatever you do, keep it simple!"

Then, the AoCs summarised the following:

Automation, when done correctly, can make a huge and positive impact in these key areas:

- **Continuous delivery pipeline** from build, testing, quality and vulnerability scans, deployment, release, and production monitoring.
- **Enforcement of governance** ranging from informal manifestos, guidelines, patterns, and practises to organisation governance and legal compliance.

- **Rapid feedback and learning** provided by artificial intelligence and analysis of audit trails, logs, and social media. Twitter, for example, is a major source for user sentiment that can be harvested and used as a deployment gate to manage the blast radius. Monitoring a negative sentiment on Twitter? Stop the bus, close the pipeline gates, analyse, learn, and pivot!

Agent 13 took a deep breath, *"Suggest that we schedule a future workshop with Automaton and a handful of your development, quality, security, and operations engineers to map out your continuous delivery pipeline.*

"Once we have metrics and understand each activity within, we can look for and remove waste, automate, and crush your lead and cycle times.

"This means less waste, less delays, and continuous and rapid delivery of value! Enable your team, get the cheese into the user's hands, eradicate cost of delay, and observe your delighted users."

Barker agreed and actioned this as another piece of work for the AoCs when they returned, which would hopefully be soon.

 To better understand the flow of value in your organisation, which can be improved in many ways, study the points previously discussed and review and try **value stream mapping** in your organisation today!

Agent 9 added before the meeting dissembled, *"Barker, on a side note – it feels odd that members of your team observe all the personality and technology clashes within yet they make no effort to encourage collaboration or resolve issues pro-actively."*

Barker and Redline nodded in acknowledgement, agreeing that they needed to encourage all, especially the Scrum Masters / Team Leads, to be more empathetic, guiding lights at sea. This was, of course, a recurring discussion with the AoCs as many had developed an appreciation of the seriousness and toxicity that silos and cliques bring to their transformation journey.

 Automate ~~Everything~~ The Automatable!

Instead of trying to automate everything, take a minute, review your processes and products, and find where it adds value to automate and integrate.

Remember; keep it **consistent**, **secure**, **manageable**, **maintainable**, and **simple** (for everyone's sake)!

Torpedo those Silos

As the AoCs prepared there final meeting with Maverick and Barker for this phase of work, they prepared a summary of information.

The DevOps mindset truly gains traction and real value when it encourages a culture of continuous learning, innovation and improvement. The AoCs had spent a significant time with Maverick, Barker and crew to develop and nurture a resilient continuous delivery pipeline. TA delivery pipeline empowers an organisation to deliver solutions with value and velocity to stakeholders and users. (We have briefly discussed the concept of value streams or VSM.)

Agent 13 described his definition of a VSM as something of value across the entire value stream from ideation to deprecation. A word of caution here, some have applied the idea of a value stream to other contexts or definitions.

Agent 77 clarified that the concept of Value Streams (VS) should not be confused with VSM and uses the following definition of a VS from Wikipedia, which is different from the Lean approach to VSM.

"Value streams are artifacts within business architecture that allow a business to specify the value proposition derived by an external (e.g., customer) or internal stakeholder from an organisation. A value stream depicts the stakeholders initiating

and involved in the value stream, the stages that create specific value items, and the value proposition derived from the value stream. The value stream is depicted as an end-to-end collection of value-adding activities that create an overall result for a customer, stakeholder, or end-user," - (Wikipedia, 2019).

Thus, when looking at VS from a business and IT / Engineering perspective and the DevOps mindset, we get a completed picture that enables both business and IT to examine value across the organisation as well as a DevOps team that is actively working, improving and collaborating with this value stream.

As the AoCs often said, *"We must all do our part to break down our organisational boundaries that create stifling silos and erode the DevOps mindset!"*

We have all created and used working integration, release, and delivery pipelines for decades. For some this may come as a shock, but pipelines are nothing new! However, the notion of a continuous delivery pipeline that empowers an effective and continuous value stream *is* new.

To support the flow of value, it is important to demolish boundaries that create **organisational** silos, such as business, engineering, operations, security, and DevOps, as well as **functional** silos, such as requirements, design, development, testing, and deployment.

"DevOps is the union of people, process, and products to enable continuous delivery of value to our end users." – Donovan Brown (Donovan Brown, 2015).

 Everyone must be fully accountable and engaged to observe, orient/analyse/inspect, and act to achieve excellence, not simply avoid errors.

In a cross-functional **team** there is no I, You or Us!

To enable organisations to deliver better products faster and succeed in a competitive market, we must foster autonomy, collaboration, alignment, accountability, decision making, and trust that is aligned with the organisation's culture and governance.

An effective and continuous delivery pipeline with fast feedback loops and the ability to pivot to changing markets is only possible when we work together as a team, without barriers, boundaries, walls or silos.

The AoCs sat down and discussed these points with Maverick. He was 100% on board and ready for the next phase of work, he just needed to convince the Overlords. As the meeting wound down, the AoCs had a few questions and points to address with him.

Agent 9 began, *"One of the core challenges in your organisation is that engineering has embraced Agile, while other parts of the business are still working with a Waterfall and gated project management."*

Maverick nodded, clarifying, *"True, I have had discussions about Agile and Waterfall with several of the department heads on many occasions. Many of these leaders do not get this mindset or are not interested. Does everyone need to be Agile to adopt a DevOps mindset?"*

Agent 77 replied, *"Part of the issue business heads use to ignore or push back on moving to Agile ways of working is that they think Agile is just for IT or engineering. That is why we have referred to Business Agility encompassing an Agile **and** DevOps mindset. Many times, it helps to have Agile coaches work with the business to help drive the mindset to complement and take advantage of it and your teams' way of working."*

Agent 13 looked out the window before adding, *"Of course, your colleagues can continue to use Traditional/Waterfall, which is like a big, fat, difficult to maneuver ship. Or they can join you and sail in a sleek aerodynamic Agile fleet, which complements and extends DevOps. However, what you will definitely need in both cases is the momentum from a heathy mindset."*

The AoCs were silent, and Agent 13 pulled a short article out of his laptop bag. This article discussed, *"having an Agile and a DevOps mindset is more effective than just doing Agile or DevOps. We need to understand and believe in what we are doing, not just go through the motions, ticking off checkboxes on a checklist."*

Agent 13 handed this printout to Maverick who appreciated hard copies he would likely refer to. Highlighted on the first page was the following:

"If you are comfortable with Lean thinking and Agile, you will enjoy the full benefits of DevOps. If you come from a Waterfall environment, you will receive help from a DevOps mindset, but your Lean and Agile counterparts will outperform you." – (AoC, 2018)

When transforming an organisation, begin with the Agile mindset, moving towards DevOps. Otherwise, you end up with two silos, namely business and engineering, divided by confusion, mistrust, mind-numbing processes, and an environment where skilled knowledge workers jump ship, sometimes without life preservers. Nobody wants that!

Maverick read the first page and nodded, *"I see, given we are IT, I can understand that a lot of the friction we are experiencing is from focusing our transformation on engineering first. If we include the business more and use their language, they may start to follow and gain agility as well?"*

"That's exactly it," the AoCs said in unison. *"Not only do you have two silos working with a different mindset, but worse, they have incompatible expectations and little trust in each other."*

Maverick shook each of the AoCs hand, hoping they would return soon.

"Great stuff," said the Agents. *"We have a little tour scheduled at the end of the day with one of the many teams you should be very proud of!"*

A healthy DevOps mindset breaks down organisational silos to foster unrestricted **collaboration**, **learning**, and **trust** across all teams.

Empower your entire organisation through a culture of shared **accountability**, **responsibility** and **trust**!

DevOps Mindset Value 5 Goal Reached

You have achieved the fifth and last of our core goals!

Inspire adoption through enthusiasm - Promote a culture of learning through Lean quality deliverables, not just tools and automation.

People are the Achilles heel of your transformation!

Umpty and many in his team were paralysed by the fear of making mistakes, worried and resistant to change. Although Automaton dazzled everyone with his automation skills, he sabotaged the continuous delivery pipeline and unsettled his colleagues with negative comments, such as "*Agile Voodoo*".

Overcoming negative employees may seem impossible, especially when you are bound to unions and labour laws. When all else fails, isolate and cherry pick them, investing in skilled and motivated people, driven by **autonomy**, **purpose**, and **mastery**.

Help guide and coach negative people, but do not leave them to their own devices - they are like a toxic substance! There are some who simply want to sink your boat, trying to suck inspiration, enthusiasm, and energy from your digital transformation like a massive hurricane of black death.

Afternoon Huddle

The AoCs were worse for wear. The super tanker, digital transformation had slowly started to change course, and its captain realised that smaller and nimble speed boats would be far easier to navigate to deliver value quickly. However, everyone, including the Agents, had realised that this was not the end and that the transformation would be a long and challenging journey.

"Now this is not the end. It is not even the beginning of the end. But it is, perhaps, the end of the beginning." – Winston Churchill

Agent 77 concluded, *"More than 70% of companies fail at transforming into adaptable, mature DevOps organisations. We can see this is about enabling sustained, measurable and business connected change. DevOps and Agile ways of working take years and require the support from leadership across the whole organisation rather than a subset or silo team. I think we can agree that we have learned a lot from coaching. I am pleased to receive feedback from the stakeholders that being an effective Agent of Chaos has really helped accelerate progress and proven value early."*

Agent 9 thought for a moment and said, *"During such a transformation, it's helpful to classify stakeholders by Influence & Interest into a quadrant. Those that are highly influential but low on interest, you keep **Satisfied**. Those that are low on both influence and interest, you **Monitor**. Those that are low on influence but extremely high on interest, you keep **Informed**. Those that are highly influential and high on interest, you keep **Engaged**."*

Agent 13 was the last to speak, *"Leaders need to realise that for a successful transformation, **listening** is essential, as is self-awareness to tune in to people's **emotions** and **motivations**. As leaders, we must **coach** and deliver structures and curated messages to disparate groups of people while simultaneously practising diplomacy to **understand** and respond **sensitively** to different ideas and feelings,* *asserting **governance** and our own ideas to lead to successful outcomes."*

Boat Inspection

To end their final day on a high note, the AoCs decided to take Maverick and Barker on a final tour of their favourite finely-tuned, high-performing team.

Fine Tuning the Water Craft – Responsibility for the HOW and WHEN

They sensed focus, passion and energy as they strolled through the team's digital war zone.

Redline and Rabbit huddled behind three monitors, troubleshooting a release pipeline issue, while Boundless quietly journaled their progress, cross-referencing product documentation. The team had surrounded their workspace with detailed process and product quick-reference posters and several enticing dashboards – almost like wallpaper! This made the AoCs very happy.

Time-boxed ceremonies around daily scrums, joint planning, collaboration, and peer troubleshooting forge an invaluable bond.

Over time, the team had also introduced a ceremony-free Friday (no daily stand-ups, demos or Retrospectives), allowing them to focus on their work, with the option to work from home. Clear signs of autonomy and trust!

Visual dashboards create a rhythmic pulse. They guide teams through their backlog, using small and steady steps, while never losing focus on quality and alignment with the leadership's vision. Delivering value and meeting acceptance criteria are common goals. Not delivering or failing a sprint seems unthinkable – although the team celebrates and learns from all sprints, as shown in the velocity chart, Figure 44.

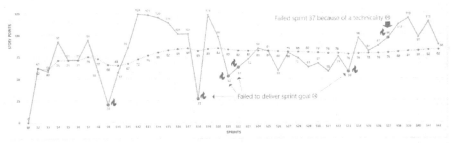

Figure 44 – Velocity Chart

The AoCs asked, *"Team, if you don't mind, we noticed you use every opportunity to highlight goals, velocity, workload and other dashboards. Why is that, and why is the velocity chart showing recent sprints exceeding the average trend line?"*

Wiggle mentioned that the team takes time to celebrate every sprint - successful **and** failed.

Redline set aside her keyboard, gathered her thoughts, smiled at AoCs, Maverick and Barker and explained the reason.

"The dashboards present a predictive, reflective, informational, and critical view of our trends and overall health. They help us focus on priority work and understand the probability of achieving our sprint goals. We also take time to enjoy nachos, wings, and other snacks as a team! It's our way to let off steam, discuss and celebrate our sprints, as well as to bond. Unscheduled 'chat and walk' strolls to the local bakery enforce a break while providing fresh air and delicious pastries to fuel the team's soul."

Knight joined the discussion, adding that the team respects and enforces a clear white line that defines the scope of work, responsibility, and autonomy. This protects them from unplanned bloat (scope creep) and ensures a realistic and sustainable workload. Everyone on the team is empowered to say "NO" when uncommitted work is thrust upon them. That work is then added to the backlog for consideration in future triage and planning ceremonies.

Redline elaborated on why their completed story points often exceed the planned or average velocity. Together with their Product Owner, they continuously groom and prioritise their backlog two to three sprints ahead. When team members complete their sprint goals, they automatically pull groomed stretch-goals from the next sprint, either creating a spike of story points in the current sprint if they finish the story or a head start in the next sprint. She smiled at Barker who had helped make this all possible.

Barker smiled back, "*Yes, I learned to lead rather than manage my team. As the Product Owner, I let the team figure out the **how** and supported their timeline for **when** they could reasonably have the feature ready!*"

It was very evident that the Product Owner, Scrum Master, and engineers plan, work, succeed, and fail as a **team**. There were no superheroes or politics, no differentiation between roles, skills, or full-time employees and contractors.

It was one happy, autonomous team with a clear purpose, working as one and trusting each other.

"Teamwork is the ability to work together toward a common vision. The ability to direct individual accomplishments toward organisational objectives. It is the fuel that allows common people to attain uncommon results." – Andrew Carnegie (Carnegie, n.d.)

What's Next?

"Well, reader, this has been an exciting and action-packed journey for all of us and Maverick's team! I bet you wonder what's next!

"There are many subjects to cover, and moving from a DevOps team that is useful for multiple projects is just one step. The next focus is on business agility, taking advantage of the DevOps mindset and Agile practises that were started and innovated on. We want to help all departments plug into Big Corp's Key Performance Indicators (KPIs), thus being flexible in delivering value continuously.

"DevOps is a challenging destination filled with rapids, rocks, sharks and many other obstacles. However, the reward can be well worth the efforts so, onward toward Security (SecDevOps) Business integration (BizDevOps)! More in-depth data integration through predictable intelligence, actions and management (DataDevOps) is on the horizon.

*"We hope you will join the AoCs on our next adventure at some other Big Corp! In the meantime, please check out supporting articles and the **Poking the Hornets' Nest** discussion on https://www.tactec.ca/ndtw-resources/ and www.opensource.com!"*

"I will re-emphasise that your transformation to a DevOps mindset is a journey with no final destination. You have entered a world of continuous observe-orient-decide-act (OODA) (Boyd, 2004), an evolution of relentless improvement and continuous

learning. There are no short cuts, and you cannot buy and install DevOps; it is a mindset! Treat anyone who tells you otherwise, or offers a product called DevOps, the same way you would treat pirates at high sea.

"It comes as no surprise that Maverick appears the most in this short adventure. If you have a leader with the energy and passion for continuous change coupled with an inspiring vision or zest for collaboration and transparency, your journey will be smooth sailing.

"Unfortunately, if you have a leader with a siloed "them/us" mindset or no tolerance for failure, you are in for some rough seas and disappointments."

"DevOps in your role/title does not translate to you <u>being</u> DevOps. Reading a book about DevOps does not make you DevOps. Using a tool named DevOps does not mean you are a DevOps expert. Being Agile does not automatically make you DevOps.

"Rather, it is how you think that makes you DevOps. Keep it simple. Keep it customer focused. If you think you are responsible for what you create; you are DevOps!"

Biographies

Authors

Brent Reed

 Agent **77**

Brent, MBCS, CDAI, CDAC, DALSM, CSM is the Founder of Tactec Strategic Solutions Inc., a digital transformation firm and PMI Disciplined Agile Partner. In the past, Brent has held senior technical leadership roles for SITA, IBM, and Heathrow Airport, along with senior global leadership roles in several start-ups in wireless tech, mobile device management and predictive analytics. Brent has worked and lived in more than 5 countries, delivering digital transformation projects, spanning many industries, such as aerospace, telecom and finance, health and public sector in over 22. Currently, he is writing his next book on Agile+ and regularly authors articles, including opensource.com. He founded and hosts the DevOps Victoria and PMI DA Guilds in western Canada, which are now global.
www.tactec.ca/team

David Hughes-Coppins

 Agent **14**

David Hughes-Coppins is an Electrical Controller in the U.K. Rail Industry. He is part of the team that created a brand-new Electrical Control Room for the Great Western Railway, producing and maintaining the 40ft Electrical Connectivity Model that governs the safe operation of its network.

When he is away from the Ops Desk, he's rock climbing or at his drawing desk, creating his own original art for children's books, comics and motorcycles.

Mathew Mathai

 Agent **9**

A non-techy at heart, he founded "a**NICHE**Inc" to help clients navigate through complex IT & Business-related change management initiatives, part time. Full time, he is a proud son and father.

www.twitter.com/aNICHEInc
www.linkedin.com/in/anishmathewmathai
www.aNICHEInc.com

Willy-Peter Schaub

 Agent **13**

Willy-Peter began his IT career in the early 1980s, during his electrical engineering studies, focusing on the BTOS/CTOS operating systems until he moved over to Microsoft technologies in the early '90s. Since then, his passion has been to investigate, research, and evangelize technology and best practises, striving for simplicity and maintainability in software engineering. Apart from sharing technology and transformation learnings in tweets, blogs, articles, and books, his varied and extreme interests include scuba diving, cycling, science fiction, astronomy, and, most importantly, his family.

www.twitter.com/wpschaub
www.linkedin.com/in/wpschaub
 www.opensource.com/user_articles/180826

References

Agent 13 & 77. (2019, May 9). *5 essential values for the DevOps mindset*. Retrieved from opensource.com: https://opensource.com/article/19/5/values-devops-mindset

Agent 13. (2018, 12 5). *Blueprint for a team with a DevOps mindset*. Retrieved from opensource.com: https://opensource.com/article/18/12/blueprint-team-devops-mindset

Agent 13. (2018, Feb 08). *Deploying new releases: Feature Flags or rings?* Retrieved from opensource.com: https://opensource.com/article/18/2/feature-flags-ring-deployment-model

Agent 13. (2019, 05 30). *Lessons Learned by an Agent of Chaos From DevOps Transformations*. Retrieved from The DevSecOps Virtual Summit: https://whitesource.brighttalk.com/webinar/lessons-learned-by-an-agent-of-chaos-from-devops-transformations/

ALM DevOps Rangers. (2020). *Azure DevOps Anti-DRIFT*. Retrieved from https://github.com/ALM-Rangers/azure-devops-anti-drift

Ambler, Lines. (2019). *Choose Your WoW*. Toronto: KDS.

Ambler, Scott. (2012-2015). *Implementing a Data Warehouse via Vertical Slicing*. Retrieved from Agile Data: http://agiledata.org/essays/verticalSlicing.html

Ambler, Scott W. (2019). *An Executive's Guide to Disciplined Agile*.

Ambler, Scott W. (2020). *DAD*. Retrieved from Disciplined DevOps: https://disciplinedagileconsortium.org/Disciplined-Agile-DevOps

AoC. (2018, 11 14). *Analyzing the DNA of DevOps*. Retrieved from OpenSource: https://opensource.com/article/18/11/analyzing-devops

AoC. (2018, Nov 14). *opensource.com*. Retrieved from Analyzing the DNA of DevOps: https://opensource.com/article/18/11/analyzing-devops

AoC. (2019, Mar 13). *Starting a DevOps transformation.* Retrieved from opensource.com: https://opensource.com/downloads/devops-transformation

AoC. (2020, 10). *Community of Practice (CoP).* Retrieved from TacTec Strategic Solutions: https://www.tactec.ca/community-of-practice-cop

AoC. (2020, 10). *Create a self formed team with post it.* Retrieved from TacTec Strategic Solutions: https://www.tactec.ca/create-a-self-formed-team-with-post-it

AoC. (2020, 10). *Create a simple assessment survey.* Retrieved from TacTec Strategic Solutions: www.tactec.ca/create-a-simple-assessment-survey

AoC. (2020, 10). *Creating effective teams with a devops mindset.* Retrieved from TacTec Strategic Solutions: https://www.tactec.ca/creating-effective-teams-with-a-devops-mindset

AoC. (2020, 10). *Improve your technical practices.* Retrieved from TacTec Strategic Solutions: https://www.tactec.ca/improve-your-technical-practices

AoC. (2020, 10). *Positive and negative characteristics of self organising teams.* Retrieved from TacTec Strategic Solutions: https://www.tactec.ca/positive-and-negative-characteristics-of-self-organising-teams

AoC. (2020, 10). *Streamline your solutions.* Retrieved from TacTec Strategic Solutions: https://www.tactec.ca/streamline-your-processes

Boone, D. J. (2007). *A Leader's Framework for Decision Making.* Retrieved from Hardward Business Review: https://hbr.org/2007/11/a-leaders-framework-for-decision-making

Boyd, J. (2004, March 10). *The Fighter Pilot Who Changed the Art of War.* Retrieved from Amazon: https://www.amazon.ca/dp/0316796883/ref=cm_sw_em_r_m t_dp_fMFLFbCTNHVD7

Brown, D. (2015, 09 01). *Technology Blog.* Retrieved from What is DevOps?: https://www.donovanbrown.com/post/what-is-devops

Bunardzic, Alex. (2019, September 26). *Mutation testing by example: Evolving from fragile TDD.* Retrieved from

opensource.com:
https://opensource.com/article/19/9/mutation-testing-
example-definition

Carnegie, A. (n.d.). *Andrew Carnegie Quotes*. Retrieved from
goodreads: https://www.goodreads.com/quotes/251192-
teamwork-is-the-ability-to-work-together-toward-a-common

David Koenig, Associated Press. (2019, June 26). *New software
glitch found in Boeing's troubled 737 Max jet*. Retrieved
from Associated Press:
https://www.metrowestdailynews.com/ZZ/news/20190626/ne
w-software-glitch-found-in-boeings-troubled-737-max-jet

Disciplined Agile. (2019). *WoW*. Retrieved from Disciplined Agile:
https://www.pmi.org/-/media/pmi/microsites/disciplined-
agile/goal-general-evolve-way-of-working-wow-
e1556188824220.jpg?v=2bd3188c-53d1-403e-81f8-
bda286033efb

Disciplined Agile. (2020). *Grow Team Members*. Retrieved from
Disciplined Agile: https://www.pmi.org/disciplined-
agile/ongoing-goals/grow-team-members

Donovan Brown. (2015, September 1). *What is DevOps?* Retrieved
from Donovan Brown: http://donovanbrown.com/post/what-
is-devops

DORA. (2014-2019). *Explore DORA's research program*. Retrieved
from Google CLoud: https://www.devops-
research.com/research.html

Driessen, Vincent. (2010, Jan 5). *A successful Git branching model*.
Retrieved from nvie.com: https://nvie.com/posts/a-
successful-git-branching-model/

Ford, H. (2014, February). *45 Quotes That Celebrate Teamwork,
Hard Work, and Collaboration*. Retrieved from
https://blog.hubspot.com/marketing/teamwork-quotes

Gene Kim, Patrick Debois, John Willis, and Jez Humble. (2016).
The DevOps Handbook. Portland: IT Revolution.

Hammant, Paul. (2017-2018). *Trunk Based Development:
Introduction*. Retrieved from trunkbaseddevelopment.com:
https://trunkbaseddevelopment.com/

Jack Welch. (2020, 10 31). Retrieved from Wikipedia:
https://en.wikipedia.org/wiki/Jack_Welch

Louis, C. (2018, March 21). *8 tips for better agile retrospective meetings*. Retrieved from opensource: https://opensource.com/article/18/3/tips-better-agile-retrospective-meetings

Marquet, L. D. (2012). *Turn the Ship Around*. New York: Penguin.

Mel Conway. (2019). *Mel Conway's*. Retrieved from Conway's Law: http://www.melconway.com/Home/Conways_Law.html

Microsoft. (2018, 3 14). *Create a pull request*. Retrieved from Azure DevOps: https://docs.microsoft.com/en-us/azure/devops/repos/git/pullrequest?view=azure-devops

Microsoft. (2019). *Visual Studio*. Retrieved from Azure DevOps: https://azure.microsoft.com/en-us/services/devops/

Microsoft. (2020). *1ES*. Retrieved from To drive engineering excellence, Microsoft dedicates team to guiding cultural change: https://azure.microsoft.com/en-us/solutions/devops/devops-at-microsoft/one-engineering-system/

Microsoft. (2020). *DevOps Self-Assessment*. Retrieved from DevOps Self-Assessment: https://devopsassessment.net/

Pink, D. H. (2010, April 1). *Drive: The surprising truth about what motivates us*. Retrieved from YouTube: https://youtu.be/u6XAPnuFjJc

PMI Disciplined Agile. (2020). *Guided Continuous Improvement (GCI): Speeding Up the Agile Kaizen Loop*. Retrieved from https://www.pmi.org/disciplined-agile/gci

Puppet. (2019). Retrieved from 2019 State of DevOps Report: https://puppet.com/resources/report/state-of-devops-report/

Puppet Labs. (2018). *State of DevOps Report*. Retrieved from Whitepapers: https://puppet.com/resources/whitepaper/state-of-devops-report

Puppet, CircleCI and Splunk. (2019). *2019 State of DevOps Report*. Retrieved from splunk>: https://www.splunk.com/en_us/form/2019-state-of-devops-report.html

Ringelmann, Maximilien. (2019, 2 2). *Ringelmann effect*. Retrieved from wikipedia: https://en.wikipedia.org/wiki/Ringelmann_effect

Schaub, Willy-Peter. (2018, May 15). *How we moved 65k Microsofties to DevOps with VSTS @ DevConf*

Johannesburg 2018. Retrieved from DevConf Johannesburg
    2018: https://youtu.be/wsWIQylZrkk

Scott W. Ambler, Mark Lines. (2019). *Choose your WOW*. Retrieved
    from Discipled Agile:
    https://disciplinedagiledelivery.com/dad-handbook/

Skelton, Matthew. (2013, 10 22). *What Team Structure is Right for
    DevOps to Flourish?* Retrieved from
    https://blog.matthewskelton.net/2013/10/22/what-team-
    structure-is-right-for-devops-to-flourish/

Snowden, Dave. (1999). *Cynefin Framework*. Retrieved from
    Wikipedia: https://en.wikipedia.org/wiki/Cynefin_framework

Tasktop. (2020). *Flow Framework*. Retrieved from Tasktop:
    https://www.tasktop.com/flow-framework

Tuckman, Bruce. (2019, July 1). *Tuckman's stages of group
    development*. Retrieved from Wikipedia:
    https://en.wikipedia.org/wiki/Tuckman%27s_stages_of_grou
    p_development

Wikipedia. (2019, August 27). *Value Streams*. Retrieved from
    Wikipedia:
    https://en.wikipedia.org/wiki/Value_stream#Purpose_of_Val
    ue_Streams

Made in the USA
Monee, IL
10 January 2024